a Practical Guide to

HUMAN RESOURCES
MANAGEMENT

JEFF STINSON
SPHR, GPHR, CCP, GRP, CBP

iUniverse, Inc.
Bloomington

A Practical Guide to Human Resources Management

iUniverse books may be ordered through booksellers or by contacting:

iUniverse
1663 Liberty Drive
Bloomington, IN 47403
www.iuniverse.com
1-800-Authors (1-800-288-4677)

Because of the dynamic nature of the Internet, any web addresses or links contained in this book may have changed since publication and may no longer be valid. The views expressed in this work are solely those of the author and do not necessarily reflect the views of the publisher, and the publisher hereby disclaims any responsibility for them.

ISBN: 978-1-4697-6083-4 (sc)
ISBN: 978-1-4697-6085-8 (e)
ISBN: 978-1-4697-6084-1 (dj)

Library of Congress Control Number: 2012902219

Printed in the United States of America

iUniverse rev. date: 3/8/2012

Acknowledgments

In writing this section, I feel like that actor onstage who has just won an award and is trying to thank the world in the few seconds allotted. I have much the same problem, as the list of those in the last thirty years who have influenced me and helped in some way to create this book would be longer than the book itself. Over the years, I have had very good and very bad bosses and role models, and I have learned as much from the bad ones as the good ones. With that, I would like to start by thanking Elise Monroe, my first boss in the private sector at Arrowhead Waters. She taught me many of the basic skills that I would use in future jobs.

Ron Bennett at Knott's Berry Farm was also an interesting role model in that he was never afraid to share feedback, much of which was not appreciated at the time. It is now, Ron, so thanks.

When it came time to "graduate" from working for human resources to working for an operations leader, I have to thank Greg Mason at Allen Bradley. In his own unique style, he showed me how to influence a business from a business and not just a human resources perspective.

Pete Loconto at BI Technologies turned me into an executive and a strategic thinker. In my first vice president position, Pete showed me the difference between a corporate leader and a site leader, and I will forever be grateful for his patience in that process.

Finally, both Greg Burden and Sherri Bovino, my current leadership, helped me understand that leadership really is about the people after all. Go figure.

Finally, nothing like this could be done without the support of my family, and particularly my wife, Diane. She has endured countless business trips and moves to help further my career, often at the sake of her own. As a teacher, she has taught me more than I can ever describe — and maybe most importantly, kept me grounded for thirty-plus years. Without her, this book would not have been possible.

Preface

//

I have been thinking about writing this book for years. In fact, the title has been in my head for the past six years — and as I sit in Cabo San Lucas, Mexico, over Christmas week sipping weird umbrella drinks, I have made up my mind to finally do it. Over the past thirty years, I have had so many good experiences leading people on several continents, working with senior leaders in the area of human resources, that I feel the need to share these experiences with you. Those thirty years have taught me that what company leaders really need is a practical book on dealing with their people issues.

As an instructor at universities around the country, I have read and used a number of excellent textbooks. They were all written by terrific thought-leaders in the field, but they all share one fatal flaw: they are of little practical use to a manager facing an immediate employee relations or other human resources problem.

For example, what do you do if your best employee tells you that he or she is leaving to go to the competition? What if one of your employees takes a public stand against one of your policies? What if someone you fire for theft hires a lawyer who sends you a nasty letter? I have yet to see a textbook deal with these real-life issues.

There are also a number of good "self help" management books that explore one area of human resources or another, from hiring to firing. These are all great and very useful, and I hope you will find this one equally so when you have finished. I have organized the book more or less in the same sequence as the employment experience.

Chapter 1 looks at the subject of how to hire the right person, from defining the job to recruiting to interviewing to making the final offer. I believe this is the cornerstone of what any leader does in his or her organization. In President George W. Bush's latest autobiography, the third chapter was entitled simply "Personnel." The first section dealt with the hiring decisions he was faced with and how he made those decisions. While none of us is likely to hire the next secretary of state, all hiring decisions are important and provide for your organization's future success or failure. They also shine a light on your decision-making ability.

Chapter 2 will discuss the best way to bring employees onboard, a process commonly known as "new employee orientation." We will talk about what makes the first ninety days critical to the success of the new hire. If done properly, these steps may keep you from having to repeat Chapter 1.

Chapter 3 will explore some possible ways to measure employee performance. While most managers look at the performance-review form as their entire performance-management system, it is simply one of several tools available to provide employees with the feedback they require to improve and sustain their performance.

Chapter 4 will look at compensation, specifically how to get the most out of what you need to pay employees to remain with the organization. While the concept of "you get what you pay for" may seem a gross oversimplification, in my experience you do get pretty much exactly what you pay for, and you need to consider what you are really looking to achieve to move your organization forward. Figure out what you want and pay for it.

Chapter 5 will examine benefits in the new "Obamacare" world. While obviously health insurance is the single largest benefit cost you will face, there are other benefits that your employees may find valuable as well, at a fraction of the price.

Chapter 6 deals with keeping employees safe from both a physical and an emotional perspective. While the workplace today is not the dangerous place it was fifty years ago and workplace deaths are less common, there are a number of safety-related issues that are unique to the twenty-first century.

Chapter 7 deals with the employee-relations issues you will encounter from time to time. While there is no magic formula for solving all of these potential employee problems, there is a sequence of events you may find useful when dealing with that uncomfortable employee problem.

Chapter 8 is actually one of my favorites: how to stay out of court. It's a constantly evolving subject and represents a chess match between you and the plaintiff's attorney.

Chapter 9 looks at the challenges of training employees on a tight budget. I have never met an employee who has received enough training, and I have found so much money wasted in this area that it can be discouraging, particularly to small-business owners.

Chapter 10 ends with a discussion of how to discipline and fire employees. I know this may be a tough way to end the employment relationship, but eventually all employees leave the organization. If we've made it through the points above well, they will leave because of retirement and not involuntarily.

Chapter 11 discusses the unique challenges of dealing with unions. Most leaders would agree that we want to prevent unions from entering our workplace, and this chapter will discuss union avoidance as well as how to deal with unions if they do get in the door.

Chapter 12 may be helpful to those of you who work internationally or are thinking of doing so. While this could be a book in itself (and may be someday), there are ideas and concepts that may help as you continue your journey overseas.

Chapter 13 takes a whimsical look at the future and explores ten areas you should think about with human resources in the years ahead. I have also included several references that may help you in your future research. These include a number of websites I have found to be very useful over the years.

Chapter 14 includes a number of humorous stories involving employee behaviors I have witnessed over the years. The title of "So you thought it was OK to what?" would be an accurate portrayal of this chapter. Also included are some funny travel stories and the things pilots and flight attendants have said to their customers that make you wonder.

I hope you find this book useful and at times humorous. If I have learned anything in the last thirty years, it is that you might as well laugh at this stuff or else you will most definitely start to cry!

Chapter 1
How to Hire Them

//

I was enjoying a perfectly lovely Monday morning when I received a phone call from a customer who was having a very bad day. One of his employees was going on a hunger strike over the way the organization treated its African American clients and did not intend to eat again until they were treated better. I'll admit, my initial thought was, *Wait a month or so, and the problem will go away.* This employee's complaint was without merit — my customer greatly respects everyone regardless of race, gender, national origin, etc. I'll go into it in more detail about this story in Chapter 6, but for now let's just say it cost a whole lot of money and time and confirmed once again in my mind the importance of making the right hire.

Most of us who have experience with hiring people understand that there is more to finding the right person than placing a newspaper ad (well, Internet these days), conducting an interview, making an offer, and hoping for the best. To hire successfully, you need to follow a process like this one:

1. Decide what skills the employee will need to be successful.
2. Write those skills down so you can refer to them later.
3. Recruit for the position in places where the right people hang out.
4. Test and/or interview candidates for the skills you need.

1

5. Make them an offer they can't refuse.

Let's look at these individually.

Decide What Skills the Employee Will Need to Be Successful

The technical name for this process is "job analysis." I have been amazed over the years by the number of leaders who have come to me and instructed me to find the "perfect" person with no idea what the perfect person looks like. So what do you need to know? Check out the following information form.

While this amount of information may look a little daunting, when finished, you have the information you need for the next step.

Position Profile			
Position Title:			
Reports To:			
Location:			
Direct Reports:	☐ Yes. If so, how many?		☐ No
Compensation/ Salary Range:		☐ Exempt	☐ Nonexempt
Benefits Package:			
Bonus Potential:			
Days/Hours:			
Travel %: US or International	☐ Yes. If so, what percentage?		☐ No
Relocation Available?	☐ Yes. If so, how much?		☐ No
Telecommuting:			
Growth Opportunities:			
Past Recruitment Efforts:			
Current Viable Candidates?			
Reason for Opening:			
Language Requirements:			
Education/Experience/Certificates/Technologies			
Education/ Degree Required:			

Industry Experience:	
Certificates:	
Technologies:	
Knowledge Required:	

Percentage	Duties and Responsibilities
%	1.
%	2.
%	3.

Anticipated Accomplishments in the first 3-12 months

1.
2.
3.

Source: Nichole DeGidio at GHRO, Global Human Resources Outsourcing

Write Those Skills Down So You Can Refer to Them Later

Again, as with most things, this has a technical name: "position profile." When finished, this will serve as a document you can use to recruit — or, if you prefer, turn over to someone else to recruit for you. Here is an example of a Position Profile for a senior administrative assistant.

POSITION PROFILE

Position Title:
Senior Administrative Assistant

Reports to:
Chief Executive Officer/President

Basic Function:
Provides administrative support to the CEO/president, including telephone support, scheduling, and communication with other departments, divisions, and companies; travel arrangements; and presentation preparation. The senior administrative assistant will also support the Real Estate, Finance and Energy divisions.

Compensation:
Target salary of $45,000 + potential bonus to be determined.

Education and Experience:
Two years of college or equivalent, with a minimum of five years of experience supporting senior leadership. Excellent English, grammar, and oral/written communication skills are a must. Excellent PC skills are also required. Must be able to work in a hectic environment with constant priority changes and adjust to various personality types.

Duties and Responsibilities:
- Ensures that all work is completed effectively; monitors the progress of work against schedules and budgets; maintains high performance standard; works effectively by using a highly collaborative style.

- Meets customer needs by developing and maintaining effective relationships with both internal and external customers and by promoting a customer-service orientation within the organization.

- Fosters relationships and a positive climate to build effective teams that are committed to organizational goals and initiatives; demonstrates flexibility in approach; is a team player.

- Creates an atmosphere in which timely information flows smoothly both upward and downward through the organization; possesses exceptional communication skills.

- Supports, manages, and initiates change within the organization, taking steps to remove barriers or to accelerate the pace.

- Actively pursues learning and self-development to enhance personal, professional, and business growth; shares learning experiences.

- Coordinates travel for the department; maintains appropriate records.

- Purchases and maintains office materials within agreed limits.

- Sorts and routes incoming and outgoing departmental mail.

- Answers telephone and gives information to callers or routes call to appropriate person; places outgoing calls, such as conference calls, if requested.

- Greets visitors, ascertains nature of business, and conducts visitors to the appropriate person.

- Reviews and gains proper approval for expense reports before going to Accounting.

- Issues check requests for department invoices (conference calls, rental cars, hotels, tradeshows, etc.).

- Schedules conference calls.

Recruit for the Position in Places Where the Right People Hang Out

I have always believed that hiring people is both an art and a science. Recruiting, however, is pure art. Many people immediately place an ad on Monster, Craigslist, or a host of other Internet job boards, and then sit back and hope for the best. Unfortunately, job boards only account for about 40 percent of all positions hired. What is the number-one source? Referrals and networking! (Source: *http://jobsearch.about.com/cs/networking/a/networking. htm.*)

Now, I am not suggesting you ignore such sites as:

- Linked In
- YAHOO! Hot Jobs
- JobCentral.com
- College Recruiter
- CareerBuilder.com
- Monster.com
- JobFox.com
- Indeed.com
- Simplyhired.com
- Jobing.com
- Net-Temps.com

Rather, I am suggesting that you need to pull out your Rolodex … oops, sorry, I dated myself, your *Outlook contacts* and start contacting people you know. For example, for the Position Profile above, I might call other CEOs, executives, and business associates, and let my Facebook and LinkedIn friends know what I'm looking for in a new hire. Keep at it, and I think you will be surprised by the results.

There are a number of other resources that can also be used to locate the right person. These include:

- Recruiters
- Temporary agencies
- Professional trade associations
- High schools, junior colleges, trade techs, and universities
- Job fairs
- Open houses
- Employee referrals

- Newspaper ads
- Government resources
- Internet database searches

Each of these sources has specific advantages and disadvantages.

Source	Advantages	Disadvantages
Recruiters (Contingency)	Contingency firms only charge when a candidate is placed, and the cost can range from 20 to 35 percent of the first year's compensation. The principle advantage is that this saves you the time and expense of running an advertisement, screening candidates, and negotiating an offer. They tend to be very good at "active" recruiting, which means they actually go into the appropriate marketplace and call candidates who may not be actively looking.	Obviously, this is an expensive convenience. Many times contingency firms will throw everyone who answers the advertisement at you to see if any of them stick.

Recruiters (Retained)	Retained search works much the same way as contingency, except you pay closer to 35 percent of the first year total compensation in three installments, the first two of which are due before anyone is hired. Retained recruiters are often used for executive and difficult-to-fill positions.	Trust is the key word here. You need to spend a lot of money on the hope that the agency will find the right person.
Temporary Agencies	The big advantage in this area is the ability to "test drive" candidates before deciding to hire them. In the past, you normally used a temporary agency for clerical and hourly positions, but now we see technical employees being hired as well.	I really like this approach, and frankly the only downside is the cost. Depending upon the deal you negotiate, you will pay the employee's salary plus all required payroll taxes and then a markup (profit for the temp agency) on top of that. This markup is very negotiable, as is the time you need to employ the individual through the temporary service before hiring. Sixty to ninety days is common.

Professional Trade Associations	Obviously, this is where the professionals you are looking for are located. If I need an accountant, why wouldn't I go to a local accounting trade association? Most have some type of placement services available for their members, even if it's just a listing of job openings on a website.	Not a lot of disadvantages, other than this won't always get you to the person who happens to be looking for a job at that moment in time. Overall, though, a good source.
High Schools	If you need entry-level employees, what better place to look? I remember once I was at a job fair at a local high school and giving away the normal "trinkets" to get the kids interested in our company. Suddenly the place emptied out, and I rushed outside to see what was going on. Guess what the US Marines did? They landed a helicopter on the football field. Now I ask you, how could I compete with this?	They are kids with little to no experience.

Junior Colleges	Junior colleges have an older population, typically, than universities do. Many students are there to learn new skills or brush up on ones, and therefore their talents may be very relevant. They may also look a bit like a trade tech.	None really. Most are glad to help you hire their students.
Trade Techs	If you need a trade, here is one great source. They are geared to help their students find jobs.	None.
Universities	Universities normally like to work with employers to find students jobs upon graduation. They prefer long-term relationships and will provide employers who make a commitment with greater access to graduating students.	These are new college graduates, full of book learning but without much practical experience. If you have the time and resources to teach them, this is an excellent source.
Job Fairs	Job fairs are a good way to get your organization's name into the community. They are normally reasonably priced and offer access to a lot of job-seekers.	Quantity is not always quality, and you will often spend a lot of time for very few good leads. There are typically a lot of "looky-loos" and those who are there for the free giveaways.

Open Houses	This is a good way to show off what a great building and organization you have. I have found this to be particularly effective when you need to hire a large number of employees.	Food and drink can be expensive, and it is difficult to control the flow of people who show up. The disadvantages are similar to those of job fairs.
Employee Referrals	I have always liked the idea of turning my entire workforce into recruiters. For the right "bounty," you would be amazed how many referrals you will get. I once paid $5,000 for a director of marketing referral that would have cost five times that amount had I used a recruiter.	My best friend is not always a good worker. What happens if I hire someone and he or she doesn't work out? This puts my reputation on the line.
Newspaper Ads	Not a lot of positives in this area unless you are in a rural community where people still spend a lot of time reading the newspaper.	Cost. Newspaper ads typically are among the most expensive types of advertising. Also, in case you hadn't noticed, it is a dying industry.
Government Resources	Quantity but not much else.	How many things does the government do well? Enough said.

Internet Database Searches	If you can afford it, this is a very nice way to reach passive job-seekers. They may have their resume in the database but not be actively looking for a job — although they could be talked into talking to you.	Cost. This can run $10,000 for an annual license. Not very cost-effective unless you are doing a lot of hiring.

Test and Interview Candidates for the Skills You Need

Once your recruiting efforts have paid off, it is time to find out if this candidate is really "the one." There are a number of ways of doing this, including paper and pencil tests, psychological profiling, and a host of skill evaluations. While many of these are excellent tools I would caution you that the federal government developed rules in the late 1970s making these kinds of tests subject to validation requirements. A discussion of validation is beyond the scope of this book so if you are interested check out the requirements in the *Uniform Employee Selection Guidelines on Selection* published by the Equal Employment Opportunity Commission in 1978.

Most of us skip all of this stuff and get right down to the interview. Interviews are more than a series of standardized questions. They need to be well planned out, with questions specifically developed to get an understanding of whether the candidate has the right skill set for the job and is a good fit for the company.

Next, the interviewer will need to be able to analyze the candidate's answers without bias and come up with an ultimate decision and/or recommendation to proceed with an offer to hire. When interviewing is done correctly, the employment interview is a powerful tool in hiring the right person. Here's a model of interviewing you might consider.

Selection Interviewing Framework

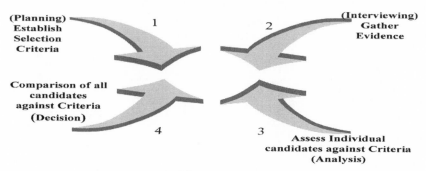

Figure 1.1

Establish Selection Criteria

When planning for an interview, it's important to consider the following pre-interview points:

1. Review the Position Profile you've prepared.
2. List some of the projects you expect the candidate to complete in the first six months. This allows you to ask questions to see if the candidate has completed such projects in the past.
3. Identify criteria on which the final selection will be made, based on the Position Profile.
4. Decide what personal attributes the candidate will need.
5. dentify the "gotta haves" and "nice to haves" that determine the right fit for this candidate. A "nice to have" is something that you would love to see the applicant possess but is not critical to their success, for example, "Coordinates travel for the department; maintains appropriate records." A "gotta have" is something that the applicant must have or they will fail. I would identify three to five such items so you can concentrate on these in the interview. For example, with our senior administrative assistant, these were our three "gotta haves":
   a. Excellent English grammar and oral/written communication skills.

b. Ability to work in a hectic environment with constant priority changes and adjust to various personality types.

c. Skill at meeting customer needs by developing and maintaining effective relationships with both internal and external customers and by promoting a customer service orientation within the organization.

Remember, a candidate must possess *all* of the "gotta haves" to succeed on the job. Unlike baseball, one out of three does not put you in the Hall of Fame.

I would also strongly recommend using the behavioral interview approach. Anyone can identify whether candidates have the skills needed to perform the essential functions of the job by reviewing his or her resume and comparing it to the job description. In my experience, I've come to the understanding that many hiring managers don't have the time or the training needed to conduct a thorough behavior-based interview to assess whether the candidate is really qualified for the job. Behavioral interviews are key to the interview process because they are designed to have the applicant take you through a situation they've experienced in the past, describe it, and then analyze it. Focus on some of these key areas.

Blast from the Past

Dr. Paul Green, a noted industrial psychologist, suggests spending your time learning what the candidate has done in the past. Research has shown that the past is the best predictor of the future. This may not always be true, but it is a much better predictor than hypothetical questions concerning what the applicant might do. So you might ask a candidate for senior administrative assistant, "Tell me about a time when you were faced with a very hectic environment. How did you meet your supervisor's priorities?"

Clear and Present Danger

Have candidates discuss what they are currently working on and their current challenges and barriers. How about this one: "Tell me about a time when you needed to provide excellent customer service."

14

Back to the Future

It's important for you to spend time understanding the candidate's short-term and long-term goals. Discussing future goals and objectives and seeing how they align with the job you're offering can indicate whether they'll be fulfilled and challenged.

Before we move any further let's take a look at some basic dos and don'ts of interviewing. First, some dos:

1. *Do* give yourself a sufficient amount of time; you shouldn't rush the process.
2. *Do* create the right atmosphere. Remember to treat others as you would like them to treat you. I once had an interview with a company that shall remain nameless, and the interviewer was eating a sandwich throughout the interview. That might have been okay, but he didn't offer me any.
3. *Do* establish an easy and informal relationship. People open up more if they feel at ease.
4. *Do* cover the ground planned and don't allow the interviewee to take control.
5. *Do* aanalyze strengths, weaknesses, and areas of interest.
6. *Do* ask open-ended questions. Simple yes and no questions don't really tell you much.
7. *Do* make judgments on the basis of fact, and try to eliminate the "gut feeling."
8. *Do* keep control over content and time.

And some don'ts:

1. *Don't* attempt too many interviews in a row. This can be a tiring experience, and the applicants will begin to run together and look alike.
2. *Don't* decide too quickly. Do you make the hiring decision in the first five minutes? Research from the Society of

Human Resources Management shows that many people do.

3. *Don't* ask multiple or leading questions. One question at a time is less confusing for everyone. Avoid saying something like, "Tell me about a time when you had multiple tasks to complete, who gave you the assignment, when was it due, how did you get it done and what did the boss think?" Yikes! Who could remember all of this?

4. *Don't* pay too much attention to isolated areas. (More on this later.)

5. *Don't* allow candidates to gloss over important facts. Drill down if you need to, and don't accept stock answers. (More on this later.)

6. *Don't* talk too much or allow candidate to ramble on. Use the 80/20 rule: the candidate talks 80 percent of the time.

7. *Don't* allow prejudices/biases to influence the process.

Gather Evidence

Now it is time to conduct the actual interview. To me, interviewing is like anything else you do, and it is better if structured. I would suggest the following sequence; it assumes a sixty-minute interview, but can be adapted to any length.

Interview Length: 60 minutes

5	25	20	10/20
Opening	Candidate Discussion	Questions	The Job (Sale)

Figure 1.2

The Opening (5 Minutes)

The purpose of the opening is to put the applicant at ease, explain the interview process, and answer any general questions. Remember, candidates who are comfortable will provide much more information

16

than those who are not. General chitchat is fine, but be sure to tell the individual what to expect for the next fifty-five minutes.

Candidate Discussion (25 minutes)

This is an opportunity for candidates to provide their background in their own words and *without* interruption. Some of you may use the "tell me about yourself" technique, but I would suggest something a bit more structured, such as: "If you could, please take me back to high school and take twenty to thirty minutes to tell me about where you have worked, your school experience, and anything else you think I should know about you." Why high school? This is generally the beginning of adulthood and is a place in time that is generally the same for most people. It is a good spot for candidates to begin their journey. Your job is to sit back and listen. Here is where the 80/20 rule really pays off. What will you learn from this question?

- Things that are important enough to the candidate to tell you about
- Reasons for leaving jobs (if they don't tell you, be sure to make a note to ask later)
- Things they did at their previous employment
- Sequence of employment (does it match the resume?)
- Detail orientation. Do they accomplish this discussion of their work history in five minutes? If so, how detailed do you think they are? It may or may not matter, because a detail orientation may or may not be a "gotta have." On the other hand, after ten minutes, are they still discussing their college experience?
- Likes and dislikes about their college experience, jobs, bosses, co-workers etc.

There is quite a bit you have learned so far, now on to the next step.

Questions (20 Minutes)

In this section, ask the candidate the various "gotta have" and "nice to have" questions you have prepared. The nice thing about this sequence is that should you decide after this step that this is the wrong candidate, skip this step and move on to the discussion of the job. This is also the time to ask questions that were generated by the candidate's discussion. For example, did they tell you why they want to leave their current employment? If not, ask them! Was there something about their relationship with a previous boss that bothers you? If so, ask them! Was there an answer that didn't make sense? Clarify it!

The Job/Sale (5-10 Minutes)

Now is the time to decide if this is someone you are serious about hiring. If not, tell them a bit about the job and the company, describe what happens next, and move on. If you are interested, here is your opportunity to "sell" the job, the company, and everything associated with the opportunity. Remember, even in a difficult economy, excellent candidates always have options.

Remember, interviewing is really gathering evidence to make a rational decision. Here are some other hints.

Do Not Be Afraid to Probe

All candidates are trying to put their best foot forward and will often gloss over important but painful issues. Does this sound familiar?

Interviewer: Why did you leave *xyz* company?

Interviewee: Well, I found a much better opportunity.

Do you accept this at face value? Why was the opportunity better? Or this:

Interviewer: Tell me about a failure you have had in your career.

Interviewee: Well, to be honest with you, I have never had one.

You buying this? It is okay to probe and dig until you are satisfied with the answer.

Allow Silence

While a little pause may be uncomfortable to you, it is important to give the candidate a chance to think of a specific example you have asked.

Ask Questions about the Past

The past is the best predictor of the future. Here are some questions that I like to use:

- What was your reason for leaving your former company? Tell me more. What did you do to change this?
- Why did you choose to work for your former company? What was the process for arriving at that decision? Did you regret making that decision? Why or why not? Has your choice of former company fit into your career goals? Do you address the issue of goals?
- What was the biggest and most important decision you have made in your life? How did you make that decision? Describe your decision-making process in that situation. Did you regret making that decision?
- Can you give me an example of how you have relied on your intuition in making a major decision? Do you ever rely on your intuition in your decision-making? Why or why not? How accurate has it proven to be? If it has not proven to be accurate, what percentage of decisions have you made using intuition?
- Can you describe a situation in which you told someone what he or she needed to hear instead of what he or she wanted to hear? How did you feel about that and why?
- Can you describe an adversity in both your personal and professional life and how you reacted? Would you act differently today? If so, how?

Do Not Use Closed-Ended or Leading Questions

Yes-or-no questions are not very valuable and can almost always be phrased in an open-ended way. Also problematic are questions like "Don't you think …" that lead candidates in the direction you want them to go. You may or may not get accurate information.

Assess All Candidates against Criteria

The final assessment consists of a comparison of all candidates against your established criteria, or the "gotta haves" and "nice to haves." It is important to remember that the successful candidate must have all of the "gotta haves" you've identified. It will do you no good to settle, because if they don't have those qualities they are not going to succeed. Whichever candidates you choose, do not make a decision based on any of the following criteria:

- Gender
- Marital status
- Family status
- Sexual orientation
- Age
- Disability
- Race
- Religion
- Color
- Any other "protected class" that may be applicable in your state. If you are not sure, search the Internet and you may be amazed at what you will find. For example, in Kentucky, smokers are a protected group.

You should make your decision based on the person best equipped with the *knowledge, skill, experience,* and *ability* to do a particular job in an exceptional manner. While one can never totally eliminate the "gut feeling," you now have some objective evidence on which to make that feeling a little more precise.

You may at some point in the process wish to even further refine your selection with the following tests:

- **Aptitude tests** to assess how well a person can learn or acquire skills and abilities;
- **Achievement tests** that measure a person's existing knowledge and skills;
- **Physical ability tests** to evaluate muscular tension, power, endurance, flexibility, balance, and coordination;
- **Personality tests** that measure an applicant's fit with the company and culture. There are a number of excellent

tests available in this area, but before you use one be sure to consult a human-resources professional.

Make Them an Offer They Can't Refuse

The final step in hiring the perfect candidate is making the offer. I certainly hope that by now you have discussed the salary range you want to pay and, to some extent, the benefits package. If not, let's hope you can come to some understanding, or the entire process may have been a waste of time.

Most savvy applicants have been taught not to discuss money until after the interview process is complete. Good for them — but very bad for you. It is better to have the parameters discussed up front so no one is disappointed at the end.

The other important point is the offer letter itself. While you may consider this step a hassle, trust me, this could save you a lot of pain later. Here is an example of a letter you may want to use:

OFFER LETTER

Date

PERSONAL AND CONFIDENTIAL

Name
Address

Dear xxxxx,

We are pleased to confirm GHRO's offer of employment for the position of senior administrative assistant. You will report to Jeff Stinson, CEO/President. Your anticipated start date is October 13, 2011. The terms of the offer are as follows:

- In this salary nonexempt position, your hourly rate will be $5,000 per month. *[Never express salaries in annual terms; various case law examples could lead someone to believe this is an annual contract.]* There is an annual bonus potential of 10 percent based on mutually agreed-on performance goals and management discretion. First-year bonus will be pro-rated if awarded prior to completion of twelve months, as may be necessary to match with established cycle.

- Employee performance will be evaluated during a probationary period. All newly hired employees will be evaluated during a six-month probationary period.
- You and any qualified dependents will be eligible for group medical/dental coverage on the first day of employment, provided an enrollment application is completed and returned within thirty-one days of your hire date.
- You will be covered under the current life and accidental-death-and-dismemberment group policy. This coverage is effective from the first day of employment. You will receive two times your annual salary to a maximum of $500,000. Additional coverage is available for you and your dependents.
- You will be eligible to participate in GHRO's 401(k) Plan under the terms and conditions of that plan. Detailed information on your company benefits will be provided at the time of your new hire orientation. The current company match is 100 percent up to the first 3 percent and then 50 percent up to 5 percent of the employee's contribution, with 100 percent vesting effective on the date of hire.
- As a condition of your employment, you will be required to provide necessary proof of legal authorization to work in the United States as required by the Immigration Reform Act of 1986. Please complete Section 1, "Employee Information," of the enclosed Form I-9 and be prepared to present the appropriate original documents on or before your first day of employment.

- You may be required to pass a background investigation for security-clearance purposes as a condition of employment. You will be required to comply with all "fitness for duty" conditions established by GHRO; it's customers, or applicable government regulations. As part of these conditions, a pre-employment drug-screening test will be required, as well as urinalysis, breath analysis, and/or blood alcohol tests as required to the extent permitted by law.
- GHRO is extending this offer based upon your general skills and abilities and not your possession of any proprietary information belonging to your former employers. Should you decide to accept this offer, GHRO requests that you do not disclose any such information to us or bring any materials belonging to your former employers.
- You agree to keep the terms and conditions of this letter confidential.

If you find this offer satisfactory, please acknowledge your acceptance by signing and returning the enclosed copy of this offer letter. If this offer is not accepted by October 1, 2011, it will be withdrawn.

Your signature will confirm:
- Your agreement with the terms of this letter.
- That these are the terms of your employment with GHRO.
- That your employment will be on an "at will" basis, which means that your employment may be terminated by you or the company at any time and for any reason.

I would like to take this opportunity to welcome you to GHRO. If I can answer any questions regarding the details of this offer, please do not hesitate to call me.

Sincerely,

Jeff Stinson
CEO/President

My signature below indicates acceptance of the offer of
employment as outlined in this letter.

_____   _____
Name   (Date)

An offer letter is valuable for a number of reasons. It sets forth
everything that the new employee needs to know prior to starting
work. There cannot be any question about salary, start date, benefits,
or requirements. Surprises really start this new relationship off on
the wrong foot and should be avoided at all costs.

Could this letter be longer or shorter? Of course. In fact, I have
seen them as long as ten pages and as short as three paragraphs.
How much information you include is of course up to you, but
the more information you provide, the less chance there is for a
misunderstanding.

Follow the hiring sequence outlined in this chapter, and the results
can be very impressive. I'd like to share a turnover success story with
you that involved taking a customer's hiring practice and revising it
to fit the standards I just described.

Does this scenario sound familiar to you? Constant hiring,
turnover of more than 20 percent per year, ridiculous workers'
compensation rates, over-the-top legal expenses, and expensive
overtime. You might be interested in seeing how these issues were
reduced by simply following a well thought out hiring process.

Imagine a 1,500-employee company that experienced the
following on an annual basis:

- Turnover of 23.2 percent

- Cost of turnover: $3,600,000
- Overtime costs of $1,300,000
- Legal fees in excess of $500,000
- Average workers' compensation cost per claim of $3,400

Not a pretty picture. We were hired to implement a process like the one I described for all nine of my customer's sites throughout the United States. In one year, the following was accomplished:

- Turnover reduced to 2.5 percent of those employees we recommended for hire
- Overall turnover cost reduced by $657,000
- Overtime reduced by $505,000 (the vacancy rate is now a record low 5 percent)
- Legal fees for those employees we recommend is $0
- Average worker's compensation cost per claim is 30 percent less.

It is *really* possible to affect this level of change in a very short period of time if you are *committed* to hiring the right people and stay true to a process. Here is how we did it.

My customer came to me in June of 2007 with real concerns about his organization's ability to hire quality staff. As a government contractor, he was limited in the wages he can pay because of tight budgets. As a result, he felt he needed professional assistance in this area. We met with his human resources team in August of 2008 and designed a talent-acquisition process designed to provide two qualified candidates for each position. It was important to ensure that our customer "bought in" to the process and had an integral part to plan in ensuring their own success. The process consists of the following steps:

1. Hiring manager identifies an open position, completes a requisition form, and forwards to the site human resources manager to secure all required approvals.

2. The approved requisition form is forwarded to the appropriate GHRO recruiter, who logs it into our applicant tracking system (ATS).
3. The GHRO recruiter initiates a conversation with the site-hiring manager to ensure that everyone is on the same page and looking for the same thing.
4. The GHRO recruiter completes the job posting and sends it to the site HR manager for posting.
5. The GHRO recruiter initiates the agreed-upon recruitment plan, including advertising as required. (One interesting side benefit of this process was the ability to secure three times the amount of advertising space given GHRO's volume purchasing power. For example, most of the sites were paying $395 for a Career Builder ad. Because of GHRO's volume, we were buying them for $110.)
6. Interested applicants apply online and are then automatically entered into GHRO's APS.
7. The GHRO recruiter does a pre-screen interview to make sure the applicant is familiar with the employer, their products, working conditions, pay, etc.
8. Assuming a mutual interest, applicants are given an online compatibility test to ensure their fit with the industry and our customer. We worked with People Talent Solutions to help us find a suitable instrument and to ensure that we validated the instrument utilizing the Uniform Employee Selection Guidelines published by the Equal Employment Opportunity Commission in 1978. After one year of experience, we have found an approximate 25 percent fail rate.
9. Assuming mutual interest, the recruiter conducts an in-depth behavioral interview designed to ensure a good fit between applicant and company.
10. Assuming mutual interest, a second online personality profile is administered. This test, also validated, is designed to measure behaviors or traits that can get in the way with success on the job. The fail rate for this test is approximately 20 percent.

11. Assuming mutual interest, a background check is completed. We have experienced a 3 percent fail rate for this part of the process.
12. Assuming mutual interest, the applicant is referred to the site for a face-to-face interview with the hiring manager.
13. Assuming mutual interest, the GHRO recruiter negotiates and prepares the offer letter and arranges for the drug screen.

I know many people have said to me, "Come on, Jeff, this will take forever." In fact, the time from requisition to presentation of candidates for the first year is as follows:

- Hourly employees: 25.5 days
- Salary nonexempt: 20.1 days
- Exempt: 20.8 days
- Supervisory/management/director: 25.7 days

Over the last several months, GHRO has taken steps to shorten the process, always with customer approval and in areas that will not affect the overall quality of the applicants presented.

This refined talent-acquisition process has saved our customer $1,700,000 in year one alone. Over three hundred employees were hired as a result — approximately 30 percent of his current workforce.

Can this level of success be duplicated in your workplace? In a word, absolutely!

Chapter 2
How to Make Them Feel at Home

//

Now that we have found the right person, we are entering perhaps the most delicate phase of the employment relationship. I am sure we can all remember those first few days/weeks of the new job. We are not sure about a lot of things. For example, who is really our boss, and what about our co-workers, and what really goes on around here? For that matter, we may not even know where the bathroom is. During this critical first ninety days, new employees will either feel at home or start to question their decision.

Statistics show that those who are on-boarded properly have a better retention rate. In fact, according to a June 2006 study conducted by the Corporate Executive Board, about 4 percent of employees leave a new job after a "disastrous" first day. The Millennials typically begin looking for their next career move after their third day on the job. With the cost of turnover as much as one-and-a-half times annual salary, this is something that needs to be and can be avoided.

Sixty years ago, due mostly to union influence, organizations invented this thing called the "probation period." The idea was simple enough. I have thirty, sixty, ninety, or 180 days to decide if you are in fact the "right" hire, and you have the same amount of time to decide if you made the correct employment decision. Of course, the balance of power is a little off. Your leaving will not likely shut down my company, but if I fire you — oh, sorry, if you fail to pass your probation period — you could end up financially devastated. Today, the courts have largely rendered this concept a thing of the past. I bring this up because I still believe the first ninety days is critical and often ignored because of this fictitious probationary period. This chapter will lay out a roadmap for those first ninety days and provide some suggestions for solidifying this new relationship.

The First Ten Days

The first ten days is what I would call the "get to know you" phase. The new employee gets to know the organization, its rules, culture, and key players, and the organization starts to make judgments about this new person's real ability. There are some who believe that we should take care of all the human-resources stuff in the first couple of days, but I would argue that there should be a balancing act between learning all of the organization's rules and being given the opportunity to do "real work."

I also believe most leaders are too busy to really bring a new hire through this process correctly. I would strongly recommend you find a mentor who can work with this new hire for the first ninety days. The mentor can work one-on-one with the employee; teaching things like "what really happens around here" and generally show the new hire around. This should be someone in the department with a vested interest in the employee's success.

I also recommend a detailed schedule be put together during the first ten days and adhered too strictly. It might look something like this:

Day 1	Morning	Free time to set up desk
		IT sets up the computer, which should be there waiting
		Learn the phone system
		Learn where stuff is — the bathroom, the break room, office supplies, etc.
	Afternoon	Meeting with the boss to learn how the next ninety days will go.
		Meeting with human resources to start that darn paperwork process

Day 2	Morning	Meet key staff the employee will be working with. I would suggest one-hour meetings with a structured agenda
	Afternoon	Finish that darn HR paperwork
Day 3	Morning	Continue meeting key staff
	Afternoon	Start the on-boarding process with a formal discussion of the organization's culture
Day 4	Morning	Continue the on-boarding process
	Afternoon	Free time to "process" what has been learned to date
Day 5	Morning	Follow up with key staff to discuss projects and expectations for the next eighty-five days
	Afternoon	Continue on-boarding process

I would continue this process for the next several days as required. Use this time to meet vendors, customers or whatever is appropriate in their situation.

A good new-hire orientation should include a discussion of the following:

- Who we are
- Our history/mission
- Our values
- Our services/products
- The organization
- Benefits briefing
- Handbook review
- Forms and other stuff
- Medical insurance
- Dental insurance
- Vision insurance
- Legal insurance
- Life/ADD
- Long-term disability
- Short-term disability
- Flexible spending account

- 401(k) and/or pension
- Tuition reimbursement
- Holidays
- Personal time off (PTO)
- The company organization
- Review of the company handbook

There are also a number of forms that you should make sure you provide the employee and have on file. Here are some examples:

CONFIDENTIAL/PROPRIETARY INFORMATION AGREEMENT AND INVENTIONS AGREEMENT

The following confirms an agreement between xxxx ("the Employee") and GHRO ("the Company"), which is a material part of the consideration for my continued employment by the Company:

1. I understand that the Company possesses and will possess proprietary information that is important to its business. For purposes of this agreement, "proprietary information" is information that was or will be developed, created, or discovered by or on behalf of the Company, or that became or will become known by, or was or is conveyed to, the Company, that has commercial value in the Company's business from not being generally known. Proprietary information includes, but is not limited to, trade secrets, computer programs, mask works, source and object codes, circuits, layouts and algorithms, designs, technology, ideas, concepts, discoveries, developments, procedures, methods, patterns, compilations, devices, know-how, processes, formulas, compositions, data, techniques, improvements, inventions (whether patentable or not), works of authorship, business and product-development plans, marketing and selling

plans, budgets and unpublished financial statements, the salaries and terms of compensation of other employees, support and training information, supplier information, customer information, manufacturing information, distribution information, cost data, pricing data, non-public bid and proposal information, and other confidential information concerning the Company's actual or anticipated business, research, or development, or that is received in confidence by or for the Company from any other person. Proprietary information also includes: [Company to insert other special proprietary descriptions] _____ _____. I understand that my employment creates a relationship of confidence and trust between me and the Company with respect to proprietary information. Finally, I also understand that it is not a violation of this agreement for the Company's employees to voluntarily discuss their pay and working conditions.

2. I understand that the Company possesses or will possess "company materials" that are important to its business. For purposes of this agreement, "company materials" are documents or other media or tangible items that contain or embody proprietary information or any other information concerning the business, operations, or plans of the Company, whether such documents have been prepared by me or by others. Company materials include, but are not limited to, blueprints, drawings, photographs, charts, graphs, notebooks, customer lists, computer disks, tapes or printouts, sound recordings, and other printed, typewritten or handwritten documents, as well as samples, prototypes, models, products and the like.

3. In consideration of my employment by the Company and the compensation received by me from the Company from time to time, I hereby agree as follows:

a. All proprietary information and all title, US patents, foreign patents, patent rights, copyrights, mask-work rights, trade-secret rights, and other intellectual property and rights anywhere in the world that I develop or receive during the course of my employment by the Company (collectively, "intellectual property rights") shall be the sole property of the Company. I hereby assign to the Company any intellectual property rights I may have or acquire in such proprietary information. I agree that all creative work prepared or originated by me, alone or in conjunction with others for the Company, or within the scope of my provision of services and/or product to the Company, and all intermediate works, such as notes and outlines and the like, that may be subject to protection under federal copyright law, constitute "work made for hire," and that upon fixation in a tangible medium of expression, all rights thereto shall be owned by the Company as the "author." At all times, both during my employment by the Company and after my employment ends, I will keep in confidence and trust and will not use or disclose any proprietary information or anything relating to it without the prior written consent of an officer of the Company. Nothing contained herein will prohibit an employee from disclosing to anyone the amount of his or her wages.

b. All company materials shall be the sole property of the Company. I agree that during my employment by the Company, I will not remove any company materials from the business premises of the Company or deliver any company materials to any person or entity outside the Company. I further agree that, immediately upon the termination of my employment by me or by the Company for any reason, or during my employment if so requested by the Company, I will return all company materials, apparatus, equipment and other physical property, or any reproduction of such property, excepting only (i) my personal copies of records relating to my compensation; and (ii) my copy of this agreement.

c. I will promptly disclose in writing to my immediate supervisor, with a copy to the president of the company and/or to any persons designated by the company, all "inventions" (which term includes improvements, discoveries, developments, methods, patterns, compilations, devices, inventions, works of authorship, trade secrets, technology, mask works, circuits, layouts, algorithms, computer programs, source code, object code, formulas, compositions, ideas, concepts, designs, processes, techniques, know-how and data, whether or not patentable) made or conceived or reduced to practice or developed by me, either alone or jointly with others, during the term of my employment. I will also disclose to the president of the company inventions conceived, reduced to practice, or developed by me within six (6) months of the termination of my employment with the Company; such disclosures shall be received by the Company in confidence (to the extent they are not assigned in paragraph 3.d., below) and do not extend the assignment made in paragraph 3.d. below. I will not disclose inventions covered by paragraph 3.d. to any person outside the Company unless I am requested to do so by management personnel of the Company.

d. I agree that all inventions that I make, conceive, reduce to practice or develop (in whole or in part, either alone or jointly with others) during my employment shall be the sole property of the Company, and I hereby assign such inventions and all intellectual property rights therein to the Company to the maximum extent permitted by Section 2870 of the California Labor Code, which provides as follows:

Employment agreements; assignment of rights

(a) Any provision in an employment agreement which provides that an employee shall assign, or offer to assign, any of his or her rights in an invention to his or her employer shall not apply to an invention that the employee developed entirely on his or her own time without using the employer's equipment, supplies, facilities, or trade secret information except for those inventions that either:

(1) Relate at the time of conception or reduction to practice of the invention to the employer's business, or actual or demonstrably anticipated research or development of the employer; or

(2) Result from any work performed by the employee for his employer.

(b) To the extent a provision in an employment agreement purports to require an employee to assign an invention otherwise excluded from being required to be assigned under subdivision (a), the provision is against the public policy of this state and is unenforceable.

No assignment in this agreement shall extend to inventions, the assignment of which is prohibited by Labor Code section 2870. The Company shall be the sole owner of all rights in connection therewith.

e. I agree to perform, during and after my employment, all acts deemed necessary or desirable by the Company to permit and assist it, at the Company's expense, in evidencing, perfecting, obtaining, maintaining, defending and enforcing intellectual-property rights and/or my assignment with respect to such inventions in any and all countries. Such acts may include, but are not limited to, execution of documents and assistance or cooperation in legal proceedings. I hereby irrevocably designate and appoint the Company and its duly-authorized officers and agents as my agents and attorneys-in-fact to act for and in my behalf and instead of me, to execute and file any documents and to do all other lawfully permitted acts to further the above purposes with the same legal force and effect as if executed by me.

f. I have attached hereto a complete list of all existing inventions to which I claim ownership as of the date of this agreement and that I desire to specifically clarify are not subject to this agreement, and I acknowledge and agree that such list is complete. If no such list is attached to this agreement, I represent that I have no such inventions at the time of signing this agreement.

g. I agree that during my employment with the Company I will not engage in any employment, business, or activity that is in any way competitive with the business or proposed business of the Company, and I will not assist any other person or organization in competing with the Company or in preparing to engage in competition with the business or proposed business of the Company. The provisions of this paragraph shall apply both during normal working hours and at all other times including, but not limited to, nights, weekends and vacation time, while I am employed by the Company.

h. I represent that my performance of all the terms of this agreement will not breach any agreement to keep in confidence proprietary information acquired by me in confidence or in trust prior to my employment by the Company. I have not entered into, and I agree I will not enter into, any agreement either written or oral in conflict herewith or in conflict with my employment with the Company.

4. I agree that this agreement is not an employment contract and that I have the right to resign and the Company has the right to terminate my employment at any time, for any reason, with or without cause.

5. I agree that this agreement does not purport to set forth all of the terms and conditions of my employment, and that, as an employee of the Company, I have obligations to the Company which are not set forth in this agreement.

6. I agree that my obligations under paragraphs 3.a. through 3.e. and paragraphs 3.g. through 3.h. of this agreement shall continue in effect after termination of my employment, regardless of the reason or

reasons for termination, and whether such termination is voluntary or involuntary on my part, and that the Company is entitled to communicate my obligations under this agreement to any future employer or potential employer of mine.

7. I agree that any dispute over the meaning, effect, or validity of this agreement shall be resolved in accordance with the laws of the State of California without regard to the conflict of law's provisions thereof. I further agree that if one or more provisions of this agreement are held to be illegal or unenforceable under applicable California law, such illegal or unenforceable portion(s) shall be limited or excluded from this agreement to the minimum extent required so that this agreement shall otherwise remain in full force and effect and enforceable in accordance with its terms.

8. This agreement shall be effective as of the date I execute this agreement and shall be binding upon me, my heirs, executors, assigns and administrators, and shall inure to the benefit of the Company, its subsidiaries, successors, and assigns.

9. This agreement can only be modified by a subsequent written agreement executed by the president of the company.

10. I represent and warrant that from the time of my first contact with the Company, I held in strict confidence all confidential information and have not disclosed any confidential information, directly or indirectly, to anyone outside the Company, or used, copied, published, or summarized any confidential information, except to the extent otherwise permitted in this agreement.

11. I acknowledge that the Company has received and in the future will receive from third parties

their confidential information subject to a duty on the Company's part to maintain the confidentiality of such information and to use it only for certain limited purposes. I agree that, during the period of my employment and thereafter, I will hold all such confidential information in the strictest confidence and not disclose or use it, except as necessary to perform my obligations hereunder and as is consistent with the Company's agreement with such third parties.

12. I represent that my employment with the Company does not and will not breach any agreements with or duties to a former employer or any other third party. I will not disclose to the Company or use on its behalf any confidential information belonging to others, and I will not bring onto the premises of the Company any confidential information belonging to any such party unless consented to in writing by such party.

13. I understand and agree that breach of this agreement (including, but not limited to, breach of any covenant or any actual or threatened misappropriation of the Company's trade secrets) shall entitle the Company to seek immediate injunctive relief without the necessity of posting any bond or proving any damages, to avoid irreparable harm to the Company's business in addition to all other legal remedies available to the Company.

14. To the extent that any of the agreements set forth herein, or any word, phrase, clause, or sentence thereof shall be found to be illegal or unenforceable for any reason, such agreement, word, clause, phrase, or sentence shall be modified or deleted in such a manner so as to make the agreement as modified legal and enforceable under applicable laws, and the balance of the agreements or parts thereof shall not be affected thereby, the balance being construed as severable and independent.

15. This agreement may be signed in two counterparts, each of which shall be deemed an original and which together shall constitute one instrument.

I HAVE READ THIS AGREEMENT CAREFULLY, AND I UNDERSTAND AND ACCEPT THE OBLIGATIONS THAT IT IMPOSES UPON ME WITHOUT RESERVATION. NO PROMISES OR REPRESENTATIONS HAVE BEEN MADE TO ME TO INDUCE ME TO SIGN THIS AGREEMENT. I SIGN THIS AGREEMENT VOLUNTARILY AND FREELY, IN DUPLICATE, WITH THE UNDERSTANDING THAT ONE COPY WILL BE RETAINED BY THE COMPANY AND THE OTHER COPY WILL BE RETAINED BY ME.

Dated: _____, 2012

_____
                    Employee

Accepted and Agreed to:

GHRO

By: _____

ATTACHMENT A

1. The following is a complete list of inventions relevant to the subject matter of my employment by GHRO (the Company), that have been made or conceived or first reduced to practice by me alone or jointly with others prior to my employment by the Company that I desire to clarify are not subject to the company's

confidential/proprietary-information agreement and inventions agreement.

    _____ No inventions

    _____ See ____ additional sheets attached.

2. I propose to bring to my employment the following materials and documents of a former employer:

    _____ No materials or documents

    _____ See ____ additional sheets attached.

Dated: _____, 2012

_____
Employee

This form protects you and ensures that the employee will keep sensitive information confidential. You will also need an Emergency Data Form.

EMERGENCY DATA INFORMATION

This form is retained in your personnel file and has limited access.

In the event of an accident or emergency during work hours, it is requested that the following person(s) be contacted on my behalf:

Emergency Contact #1

Name: _____

Address: _____

Work Phone: _____Home Phone: _____

Relationship: _____

Emergency Contact #2

Name: _____

Address: _____

Work Phone: _____Home Phone: _____

Relationship: _____

Medical Information

Family Physician: _____

Address: _____

Business Phone: _____

Special information (i.e. diabetic, rare blood type, epileptic, contact lenses, etc.)

_____

Employee Signature: _____

Date:_____

    An oft-overlooked part of the employee new-hire process that in fact should be done during the interview process is the application form. The one presented is a bit different, because it ties the required information to the company's core values.

GHRO, GLOBAL HUMAN RESOURCES OUTSOURCING (GHRO)

Who We Are and What We Value

Thank you for your interest in applying to work for GHRO.

What is our culture?

Innovative professionals bound by our core values. We believe in making a positive impact with our service, support, and training, and have been doing so since 1919. The growth and development of our people are the keys to our success.

Based upon our culture, we have established core values that define who we are and how we operate. What are our core values?

- Individual accountability
- Personal growth
- Integrity
- Respect
- Commitment
- Safety

By completing this application, you will help us to learn as much as possible about you. One of our core values is *integrity.* We trust that you will be honest about what you provide on this application or during your interviews. Please do not withhold any information that, if disclosed, would affect your application unfavorably.

Our application process is designed to help both of us decide whether you should join the GHRO Team. Now that you know something about our culture and core values, please help us learn about you.

GHRO CORE VALUE
EMPLOYMENT APPLICATION

Getting to Know You:

Name
_____

(Print) Last   First   Middle

Present Address
_____

Street and Number   City   State Zip Code

How long have you lived there? _____
_____

Years_____   Months_____

Previous Address _____
_____

Street and Number   City   State   Zip Code

How long have you lived there? _____

Telephone No._____

Social Security No. _____

Have you ever worked for this Company before? [ ] Yes [ ] No

If yes, please give dates and position: _____
_____
_____
_____

What are you passionate about?
_____
_____
_____

Where Have You Worked?

This section of the application highlights your past experience and our core values of *individual accountability* (where you worked and why you left) and *growth* (continuous learning).

Present or Last Employer	Employed	Pay	Your Title or Position	Exact Reason for Leaving
Address _____	From (mo/yr) _____	$ _____ Start	_____	_____
City, State, Zip Code _____		$ _____ Final	Name and Title of Last Supervisor _____	_____
Telephone _____	To (mo/yr) _____		What is the most important contribution this company provided for you? _____	_____
What is the most important contribution you have made to this company? _____				_____

46

Present or Last Employer	Employed	Pay	Your Title or Position	Exact Reason for Leaving
Address _____	From (mo/yr) _____	$ _____ Start	_____	_____
City, State, Zip Code _____	To (mo/yr) _____	$ _____ Final	Name and Title of Last Supervisor	
Telephone _____			_____	
What is the most important contribution you have made to this company? _____ _____			What is the most important contribution this company provided for you? _____ _____	

47

Present or Last Employer	Employed	Pay	Your Title or Position	Exact Reason for Leaving
Address _____	From (mo/ yr) _____	$ _____ Start $ _____ Final	_____	_____ _____ _____ _____ _____ _____
City, State, Zip Code _____ Telephone _____	To (mo/yr) _____		Name and Title of Last Supervisor _____	
What is the most important contribution you have made to this company? _____			What is the most important contribution this company provided for you? _____ _____	

Present or Last Employer	Employed	Pay	Your Title or Position	Exact Reason for Leaving
Address	From (mo/yr)	$_____ Start		
City, State, Zip Code		$_____ Final	Name and Title of Last Supervisor	
Telephone	To (mo/yr)			
What is the most important contribution you have made to this company?			What is the most important contribution this company provided for you?	

Have you ever been terminated or asked to resign from any job? [ ] Yes [ ] No
If yes, please explain circumstances: _____

What Is Your Background?

This section highlights our core value of *personal growth*. We believe in continuous learning. Please include personal as well as professional programs.

EDUCATION

School Name	Years Completed (Circle)	Diploma/ Degree	Describe Course of Study or Major	Describe Specialized Training, Experience, Skills, and Extracurricular Activities
Elementary:	4 5 6 7 8			
High School:	9 10 11 12			
College/University:	1 2 3 4			
Graduate/ Professional:	1 2 3 4			
Trade or Correspondence:				
Other:				

50

Can Your Team Count on You?

How many days of work have you missed in the last three years for reasons other than paid holidays and vacation?

Year   Number of Days

Year   Number of Days

Year   Number of Days

Compliance With the Law:

This section highlights our values of *integrity, individual accountability, respect,* **and** *safety.* **Your past violation of criminal laws or other circumstances could impact your ability to work with our team members and clients.**

Have you ever pled guilty or "no contest" to, or been convicted of, a misdemeanor or felony?   [ ] Yes [ ] No
If yes, please give the date(s) and details:

Have you been arrested for any matters for which you currently are out on bail or on your own recognizance pending trial? [ ] Yes [ ] No

If yes, please give the date(s) and details:

Note: Answering "yes" to these questions does not constitute an automatic bar to employment. Factors like age and time of the offense, seriousness and nature of the violation, and rehabilitation will be taken into account. (Do not include minor traffic infractions, convictions for which the record has been sealed or expunged, any conviction for which probation has been successfully completed or otherwise discharged and the case has been judicially dismissed, referrals to and participation in any pretrial or post-trial diversion programs, and marijuana-related offenses that occurred over two years ago in answering these questions).

How Are You Viewed by Others?

Personal References
Please list persons who know you well other than your relatives.

Name	Occupation	Address (Street, City, and State)	Telephone Number	Number of Years Known

Thank you for completing this application.

Going Forward:

We will evaluate your answers and contact you if we want to learn more about you through a face-to-face interview.

We want to make sure that you understand that any team member must pass a drug test prior to joining GHRO. This is part of our core value of maintaining a safe workplace by establishing a drug-free zone.

GHRO also believes that if there is any dispute that may take place as a result of your seeking employment with GHRO or employment by GHRO, it will be decided by binding arbitration before a retired judge. We believe that the court system does not provide an effective method to efficiently resolve differences that may come up between GHRO and you. This is why all disputes that may arise involving GHRO, its managers, and its employees, vendors, and clients will be resolved through binding arbitration under the Federal Arbitration Act, in conformity with the procedures of the Federal Rules of Civil Procedure. GHRO will pay for all expenses unique to the private arbitration forum. This agreement covers all disputes, including those based on state and federal discrimination laws and any claims of tort, contract, or other issues between you and GHRO. You and GHRO will not arbitrate any issues that are covered by the National Labor Relations Act, the State Workers' Compensation Act, Unemployment Compensation claims, any claims that are initially filed with either the state discrimination agency or the Equal Employment Opportunity Commission, or as otherwise required by state or federal law. If you choose to pursue a claim with a state or federal agency, following the exhaustion of such administrative remedies, that claim will be decided by the retired trial judge selected by you and GHRO, who will provide a written opinion that sets forth the essential findings and conclusions for any award. GHRO believes that the use of our core values should eliminate the need for binding arbitration; however, the use of binding arbitration is a condition of employment with GHRO, except where prohibited by law. *It is important that you understand that both you and GHRO are giving up the right to a jury trial of any claim that you or GHRO may have against each other.*

If you have any questions regarding this statement and the arbitration agreement, please ask a **GHRO** representative before signing, because by signing, you acknowledge that you have read the agreement, understand it and agree to its terms. Do not sign below until you have read the agreement above.

_____

Signature of Applicant   Date

Some organizations are covered under Federal Affirmative Action rules and as such may need to have potential and current employees provide the following:

INVITATION FOR EMPLOYEES TO SELF-IDENTIFY

GHRO is a federal contractor subject Title 41, Part 60 of the Code of Federal Regulations, Equal Employment Opportunity, which requires us to develop and implement an affirmative action program to ensure Equal Employment Opportunity and Non-Discrimination. Our affirmative-action program includes the three affirmative-action plans listed and summarized below. If you feel that you would be covered under one or more of these plans, you are invited to voluntarily identify yourself by indicating the plan(s) from which you would like to benefit and by signing this form.

1. **Females, Minorities, and other Protected-Class Employees.** Executive Order 11246 requires federal contractors to undertake affirmative action to employ and advance qualified individuals, without regard to race, color, religion, gender, or national origin. We take affirmative action to ensure that females and

minorities in our workforce are approximately equal to the availability of qualified females and minorities in our labor area. If you feel you would be covered under this plan, and you would like to benefit under our affirmative-action program, we would like to include you in it. You are invited to identify yourself by checking the statement on the reverse and signing this form.

2. **Individuals with Disabilities**. Section 503 of the Rehabilitation Act of 1973, as amended, requires federal contractors to undertake affirmative action to employ and advance in employment-qualified individuals with disabilities. If you are an individual with a disability, we would like to include you in our affirmative action program for recruiting, employing and advancing individuals with disabilities. You are invited to identify yourself by checking the statement on the reverse and signing this form. If you are an individual with disabilities, it would assist us if you tell us about: (1) any special methods, skills, and procedures that qualify you for jobs you might not otherwise be able to do because of a disability, so that you will be considered for any positions of that kind; and (2) the accommodations we could make that would enable you to perform the job properly and safely, including special equipment, changes in the physical layout of the job, elimination of certain duties relating to the job, and provision of personal assistance services. This information will assist us in placing you in an appropriate position and in making reasonable accommodations for your disability. Information you submit about your disability will be kept confidential, except that: (1) supervisors and managers may be informed regarding restrictions on the work or duties of individuals with disabilities, and regarding necessary accommodations; (2) first-aid and safety personnel may be informed, when and to

the extent appropriate, if the condition might require emergency treatment; and (3) government officials engaged in enforcing laws administered by OFCCP or the Americans with Disabilities Act may be informed. We will use the information provided only in ways that are consistent with applicable law and regulations.

3. **Veterans.** The Jobs for Veterans Act and the Vietnam Veterans Readjustment Act require federal contractors to take affirmative action to employ and advance qualified veterans in the following categories:

   a. Recently separated US Armed Forces Veterans with a discharge date within three years of current date

   b. Other US Armed Forces protected veterans — individuals who served active duty in a war, campaign, or expedition for which a medal was authorized

   c. US Armed Forces service-medal veterans only — individuals who participated in a military operation or which an Armed Forces service medal was authorized.

   If you are a special disabled veteran, it would assist us if you tell us (1) about any special methods, skills, and procedures that qualify you for positions you might not otherwise be able to do because of your disability, so that you will be considered for any positions of that kind, and (2) the accommodations we could make that would enable you to perform the job properly and safely, including special equipment, changes in the physical layout of the job, elimination of certain duties relating to the job, and provision of personal assistance services. This information will assist us in placing you in an appropriate position and making accommodations for your disability.

Information you submit about your disability will be kept confidential, except that: (1) supervisors and managers may be informed regarding restrictions on your work or duties, and regarding necessary accommodations; (2) first-aid and safety personnel may be informed, when and to the extent appropriate, if the condition might require emergency treatment; and (3) government officials engaged in enforcing laws administered by OFCCP or the Vietnam Veterans Readjustment Act may be informed. We will use the information you provide only in ways that are consistent with applicable law and regulations.

Voluntary Disclosure. Providing this information is voluntary. If you decide not to provide it, you will not experience any adverse consequences because of your decision. If you would like to be considered under our affirmative-action program, please tell us. You may inform us of your desire to benefit under the program at this time and/or at any time in the future. If you choose to voluntarily disclose this information and wish to be considered under our affirmative-action program, please checkmark statement one or more of statements 1, 2, or 3 below, and sign your name. If you do not feel you would be covered under one of these plans, or do not wish to disclose information at this time, checkmark statement number 4 below and sign your name, or leave the entire form blank.

If you would be covered by our affirmative-action plan and do not wish to be considered under it at this time, you may request to be considered at any time in the future.

Gender: ☐ Female
☐ Male

Race/Ethnicity: ☐ Hispanic or Latino
☐ White
☐ Black or African American
☐ Native Hawaiian or Other Pacific Islander
☐ Asian
☐ American Indian or Alaskan Native
☐ Two or more races

Veteran : ☐ Recently Separated US Armed Forces Veteran
☐ Other US Armed Forces Protected Veteran
☐ US Armed Forces Service Medal Only Veteran

☐ We make reasonable accommodation for individuals with disabilities. Please check the box to the left if you wish to request reasonable accommodation to complete the application.

☐ I feel I would be covered by your affirmative-action plan and wish to be considered under it.

☐ I do not feel I would be covered by your affirmative-action plan

Signature: _____ **Date:** _____

From time to time, human resources may receive calls to verify employment-related information. As such, having this form on file will expedite that process.

AUTHORIZATION TO RELEASE PERSONAL INFORMATION

I hereby authorize GHRO:

_____To provide my date of hire, salary, social-security number, and title to anyone who may call regarding verification of employment.

_____ To release only the specific type of information listed below to anyone who may call regarding verification of employment.

_____

_____

_____

_____ Not to release any personal information on me whatsoever.

_____
Signature

_____
Printed Name

_____ / _____ / _____
                              Date

Please remember that every state is a bit different. Check with your state employment department for your state's specific requirements.

My thanks to Northwestern University for this comprehensive checklist, and I would recommend you create something similar to ensure that you don't forget key items.

NEW EMPLOYEE ON-BOARDING CHECKLIST

This checklist is designed to assist with the department's orientation process. On boarding is a long-term process that begins before an employee's start date and continues for at least six months. This checklist is organized chronologically and helps hiring managers prepare for the arrival of new employees. Once an employee starts, he/she can work together with the hiring manager and an on-boarding peer* to complete the checklist. The hiring manager may add additional activities that are relevant to the new employee's area. Internal transfer employees may omit items that are not applicable.

*An on-boarding peer is a peer to the new employee who can assist in the on-boarding process and be a "go to" person as directed by the manager.

Pre-Arrival

Print out New Employee On-Boarding Checklist, review, and customize.
Confirm offer letter sent to new employee either by Human Resources or hiring manager.
Call to officially welcome the new employee after confirmation of acceptance.
Provide new employee with a contact in the event of a question or issue.
Create an on-boarding schedule for the new employee.
Assign an on-boarding peer* for new employee's first two months on the job.
Schedule new employee to attend orientation within the first two weeks of start date. No advance registration is required. For time and location, go to *http://www.northwestern.edu/hr/training/ newemployee.html.*
Send temporary parking permit to new employee (before hired into the HRIS system). A permanent parking permit can be obtained from the parking office once a new employee is hired into the HRIS system.
For Evanston, please call x. For more information, visit *http://www.northwestern.edu/up/parking.* (To obtain a temporary parking permit, bring a memo on Department/School/Northwestern University letterhead indicating the new employee's department, position title, and start date to the Parking Services office)
For Chicago, please speak to your department Parking Administrator or call the Parking office at x. For more information, visit *http://www.univsvcs.northwestern.edu/Chicago_parking.*
Set up computer, phone, login password, and office supplies.
Send an announcement via e-mail to the department announcing the new hire and start date.

To order business cards and nameplate

Business Cards	Nameplate
Triangle Printing	University Services, Printing & Duplication

To obtain a NetID for the new employee up to thirty days before the date of hire:

(New employees must be hired in HRIS to get a NetID in order to sign-in to HRIS Self Service for Benefits Enrollment. For additional NetID automation information, visit *http://www.northwestern.edu/hr/hris/netid/ index.html*)

The new employee completes the Personal Data Form and faxes it back immediately to the respective HR fax number for each campus as indicated on the offer letter. Download the form at *http://www.northwestern.edu/hr/payroll/PersonalDataForm.pdf*.
When the NetID is created, the NetID coordinator (usually the department manager) will be notified by e-mail.
NetID coordinator provides the NetID, e-mail account, and password information to the new employee, who then activates the NetID at *http://www.northwestern.edu/facstafflogin*.

Additional activities to complete if applicable:

Union workers — contact HR manager of Facilities Management.
Send nonresident alien information web links to new employee and request he/she to fill out the forms (if applicable). Go to *http://www.northwestern.edu/international* and click on Faculty and Staff.

62

Nonresident alien — contact the International office at http://www.northwestern.edu/international. Contact Payroll at x (Evanston) or x (Chicago) to register to use the Foreign National Information System. For more information, visit http://www.northwestern.edu/hr/payroll/nonresidentinfo.html.

Arrival

1st Day	Who Initiates
Go to HR office (Evanston — 720 University Place; Chicago — Abbott Hall) to complete W-4, I-9 and Personal Data Form, sign Employment Application, and receive Staff Handbook and benefits packet.	Employee
Remind new employee to complete the online benefits enrollment via eBenefits within the first thirty-one days of employment. (Must have NetID and password.)	Hiring Manager

Department On-Boarding

Introduce to co-workers.	Hiring Manager
Distribute assigned key and/or access card to office.	Hiring Manager
Discuss procedures for scheduling time off and unexpected absences.	Hiring Manager
Review work schedule, pay schedule, and overtime policy (if applicable).	Hiring Manager
Review appropriate attire for workplace or lab.	Hiring Manager
Go over phones, fax, copier, and office supplies.	Peer
Provide NU Computer Orientation at desk (computer sign-in, shared drives on network, e-mail, Meeting Maker, school/department's website).	Peer
Give a department tour (place to hang coat, washroom, water fountain, vending machine, pantry/kitchen, refrigerator, emergency exit, parking space).	Peer

	Arrange a welcome lunch for new employee.	Hiring Manager and / or Peer
Within First Week		
	Activate NetID online if you have not done so at *http://www.northwestern.edu/facstafflogin*.	Employee
	Bring photo identification and NetID to obtain WildCARD from the WildCARD office in Norris for Evanston (underground level) and Abbott Hall, Room 100 for Chicago. (Please verify NetID is in the system before going.)	Employee
	Obtain permanent parking permit from the Parking office @ 1819 Hinman Avenue, Evanston or @ Abbott Hall, Room 100, Chicago (prior department approval required for Chicago parking). Must have NetID.	Employee
	Sign up for direct deposit and update online directory in HRIS-Self Service website (must have NetID and password) at *https://nuhr.northwestern.edu/*.	Employee
	Sign up for CTA or RTA benefits programs (for CTA train and shuttle, and Metra commuters), if desired, at *http://www.northwestern.edu/hr/payroll/transit.pdf*.	Employee
Communicate Job Expectations and Review Departmental Procedures		
	Review job responsibilities, competencies, and expectations.	Hiring Manager
	Review performance feedback and appraisal process using Performance Excellence process. Visit *http://www.northwestern.edu/hr/training/perfex.html*.	Hiring Manager
	Review department's mission, strategy, values, functions, policies, and procedures; organization of the department; critical members of the department; departmental staff directory, department calendar, confidentiality of information; emergency regulations; and health and safety training.	Hiring Manager

Review university standards for business conduct (nondiscrimination; no smoking, drug and alcohol; no tolerance of workplace violence; sexual harassment prevention and resolution).		Hiring Manager
Review department safety plan.		Hiring Manager
Training (as applicable):		
CUFS training.		Employee
HRIS training. Go to HRIS Self Service at *https://nuhr.northwestern.edu*. (Under the Learning and Development folder, click Request Training Enrollment and then click Search by Course Name. Type in HRIS and hit search; all scheduled courses for HRIS will be listed.)		Employee
eRecruit training. Sign up at *http://www.northwestern.edu/hr/hris/erecruit/index. htm*		Employee
Electronic Time Entry System (ETES) computer-based training (CBT) (for biweekly staff and temporary employees only).		Employee
Other workshops and trainings: *http://www.northwestern.edu/hr/training*.		Employee
Within 2 Weeks		
Attend New Employee Orientation, Part 1: benefits, work schedule, payroll, university resources, ethics and compliance, IT security, campus safety, and parking.		Employee
Schedule new employee to attend New Employee Orientation, Part 2 two to three months into employment. (Advance registration required. Please visit *http:// www.northwestern.edu/hr/training/newemployee.html*).		Hiring Manager
Schedule weekly or monthly meeting to touch base with supervisor.		Employee

65

	Responsibility
Overview of budget and finance procedures and policies (if applicable).	Hiring Manager
Facilitate enrollment in the University Business Processes Workshop(s) related to job: Introduction to University Business Processes, Acquiring Goods and Services, Accounting and Reporting Processes, Effective Business Operations (as applicable). Sign up online at *http://www.northwestern.edu/hr/training/business.html*.	Hiring Manager

Within First Month

	Responsibility
Enroll for benefits via electronic eBenefits system within thirty-one days of hire date.	Employee
Review and clarify performance objectives and expectations after the first month.	Hiring Manager
Set up brief meeting with department head (director or vice president).	Hiring Manager
Register for New Employee Orientation, Part 2.	Employee

During First Ninety Days

	Responsibility
Attend New Employee Orientation, Part 2: Hear from a Northwestern senior leader about the university's current state and future direction; attend Standards for Business Conduct and Performance Excellence workshops for managers and staff; and meet fellow new employees.	Employee
Review and discuss the new staff member's performance objectives.	Hiring Manager

Fifth and Sixth Month

	Responsibility
Review performance objectives and progress.	Hiring Manager
Discuss training completed and training planned for the future.	Hiring Manager

Annual Performance Review

	Conduct annual performance review.	Hiring Manager
	Set objectives for the coming year with employee.	Hiring Manager

Once complete, this checklist should be signed by both the staff member and the supervising staff or faculty member. A copy should be provided to the staff member with the original filed in the department staff member's file. Please contact your Human Resources consultant with any questions.

Staff Member's Name (Please Print) _____

Job Title _____   Hire Date _____

Staff Member's Signature _____   Date _____

Supervising Staff or Faculty Member Signature _____

The Next Ten Days

The new employee has now had two weeks to become acclimated to the company culture and key staff, so it is now time for some constructive activity.

In the Position Profile section of Chapter 1, there is a section for anticipated accomplishments for the first three to twelve months. If you have given this some thought, now would be the time to go over these projects with your new hire. These projects should be meaningful and contribute to the overall organizational goals. They should also be small enough in scope to allow you to evaluate the work during the so-called "probationary" period.

That's it. At this point, we should have a great employee who has shown an ability to make a meaningful contribution to the organization. Now let's move down the path of measuring their long-term performance.

Chapter 3
How to Measure a New
Employee's Performance

//

At this point, we are pretty sure we have hired the "right" person, have made sure the new employee was properly oriented and made to feel at home, and have seen some early work. Now the process of performance management really begins.

There are leaders who believe that the "performance review" is all that is required of the performance management system. After all, they fill out the forms, spend time discussing the review with the employee, and establish goals for the following year. Isn't that it? It very well may be, if your system has no desire to tie the employee's goals to the overall goals of the organization. If the goal is to simply measure an employee's performance vs. a series of pre-determined goals, then yes, you are done. If, on the other hand, you want to tie everyone in the organization to the goals of the organization, more work will need to be done.

Designing Smart Goals

The first step in any employee review process should be the development of clear and achievable organizational goals. This is more than just sales and revenues, even though those are critical. Whatever organizational goals you decide are important, they must be communicated throughout the organization, even down to the lowest level. From here, you can start to establish employee goals that are "smart." Here is what I mean by smart goals:

Goals need to pass the SMART test.

Specific
Measurable
Action oriented
Realistic
Time frame

Let's look at each of these in more detail.

Specific

Define precisely the objective or outcome you want. Provide enough detail so that there is no indecision as to what exactly the employee should be doing. A goal to "improve quality" means well but does not meet the *specific* goal test. A much better goal would be: "Improve the quality of my reports to be 95 percent error free." Goals should not restate the employee's job description. A goal is something that brings an improvement to the department and the entire organization.

Measurable

Define how you will know when the employee has attained the goal. The goal should be such that when completed, there is tangible evidence. Use one or more of the following to help make the goal measurable: numbers, percentages, completion time, dates, and what completion it will look like. An example: "Distribute the monthly financial reports by the fifth day of each month 100 percent of the time."

Action Oriented

State the goal using an action verb — such as *improve, reduce, start,* and *complete* — to describe the steps required.

Realistic

Confirm your belief that the goal is indeed possible. Better to plan fewer things and be successful than plan too many things and be unsuccessful. Success breeds success! For most of us, three to six significant goals are enough. Three to six good goals will do more for you and the organization than fifteen smaller goals. Confirm that employees feel these goals are realistic, or they may give up and not try to achieve them.

Time Frame

Set a deadline for reaching the goal. Here's a tip: If your goal is large or complex or has a completion date that is far off in the distance, set interim goals with deadline dates along the way. This way, employees will see their successes.

Goals need to be clearly worded. Effective, well-written performance goals contain these four elements: To (action verb)+(results)+by when (date)+standard (cost or quantifier). For example, "To increase sales in the department by 30 percent by December 15, 2011, with an increase in overhead of less than $5,000." That seems pretty clear, doesn't it?

Once you and the employee agree on the goals, the process should include frequent feedback to make sure he or she is on track. I would suggest quarterly conversations, but depending on how complex the tasks and how skilled the employee is, more frequent feedback may be necessary.

Effective Written Feedback

While I did imply that the review form was not the actual performance-management system, I don't want to forget how important it is to provide the employee written feedback. There is no "perfect" review form, and your company culture will dictate how best to do this, but let me share some thoughts on what any good form should contain.

Any form you choose should include the following information:

• Employee name

- Employee title
- Current department and/or location
- Employee date of hire
- Date that the performance review was completed
- The review period — normally a calendar year but in some cases, it could be another time frame.

More detailed sections like the ones below that give the employee specific guidance, information, and recommendations should also be included.

Position Outcomes

In two or three sentences, list the expected outcome of the employee's position. Why does this position exist? You will want to review the employee's job description as a frame of reference. Feel free to attach this as a reference document.

Accomplishments

Determine the top three or four areas in which this employee has made the greatest contribution. Examples include:
- Lowered workers' compensation costs by 15 percent
- Improved site quality scores by 2 percent
- Reduced site absenteeism by 10 percent
- Developed a safety incentive program
- Increased student retention rates by 5 percent

Please review the employee's quarterly and annual goals for the year to determine what the individual has accomplished. What is important to remember about accomplishments is that there needs to be an impact on the department, group, or company. Accomplishments are more than the day-to-day tasks we are all engaged in; they go beyond the everyday scope of the employee's position. Some other accomplishments may include the employee implementing a cost savings idea or a process improvement.

Strengths

Think about the things that this individual does really well. When you think of this person, what three positive qualities come to mind? Why? Determine the top three and think of a situation in which this employee demonstrated these skills on the job. List the strengths along with the specific examples that demonstrate these strengths. For example:

- Completes projects on time with a tremendous sense of urgency: "All of your monthly status reports were turned in on time."
- Has a great attention to detail and accuracy: "Your contract proposals are always on time, and I have not found any errors."
- Identifies problems quickly and finds solutions: "You were able to develop a solution to the missing equipment issue, and you did so in less than a week."
- Has very good creative skills: "The proposal you prepared for the customer was very creative and provided for additional opportunities in the future."
- Takes accountability for his or her actions: "Even though the budget you submitted was late, you accepted responsibility for the delay and worked overtime to rectify the problem."
- Handles conflict in the appropriate manner: "You have shown the ability to confront individuals when they have violated our core values."

As we saw in the interviewing process, specific examples help the employee understand what you are trying to say. The more specific the examples you provide the better.

Areas for Improvement

What are the skills it takes to do this job? Does this person have room for improvement in these areas? If so, list them. Also, think in terms of growth and challenge for this employee. Does this employee have the skills needed, or could he or she use some training to get there? Discuss these areas as opportunities for career growth with the employee. Again, provide specifics. It is also important that the employee understand how serious the area for improvement is. There are three categories to consider.

Low

The employee is basically doing a very good job. This area of improvement might help the employee improve from a "successful" to "excellent" rating on the next performance review.

Moderate

The employee may or may not be doing a good job. If not corrected, this area of improvement could move the employee from "successful" to "marginal" on the next Performance review.

Severe

If not corrected, this area of improvement could lead to the employee's eventual separation from the company.

Employee Personal/Professional Growth Plan

The purpose of the Employee Personal/Professional Growth Plan is to provide employees with a specific plan to help them achieve personal and professional growth. From an organizational perspective, you should consider the following:

- Where is the employee currently in the organizational structure?
- Where would the employee like to progress in the next twelve to thirty-six months?
- What specific opportunities within the organization can you provide that will allow the employee to meet this goal?
- What specific training opportunities outside of the organization can you provide?
- What is expected of the employee in terms of commitment?

Allow the employee to discuss this plan with you ahead of time. You should allow the employee to complete the "comments and suggestions" portion shortly after the overall performance discussion.

Company Values

Every organization has different values. My company's values are listed here as an example.

Individual Accountability

Employees are expected to:

- Be responsible for their actions.
- Provide timely responsible feedback.
- Follow through with commitments.
- View obstacles as opportunities.
- Be proactive.
- Have fun.

Our operating principles:

- Always seek closure before moving on and learn from our mistakes so we don't repeat them.
- Be proactive, not reactive. Act now — don't wait until a crisis to ask for help.
- Provide timely responsible feedback that focuses on the issue, not on the person.
- Commitments count, both up and down.
- You are personally responsible to raise your hand when something is wrong.
- Keep a positive attitude and remember to have fun.

Growth

Employees are expected to:

- Learn to let go.
- Embrace change.

- Celebrate success.
- Continuous learning.
- Promote innovation.

Our operating principles:

- There are no bad ideas, just ideas that don't fit right now.
- There is a difference between an honest mistake and a deliberate misdeed.
- We work as a team, share our knowledge, build on our current capabilities, and foster growth in our people.

Integrity
Employees are expected to:

- Be trustworthy.
- Value honesty at every level.

Our operating principles:
- Open, clear, concise, and honest communication is required across the board, especially in regard to changes and information that impacts others.
- Personal integrity is expected at every level.
- Trust each other, assume right intentions, and keep focused on the big picture.

Respect
Employees are expected to:

- Listen for meaning.
- Be approachable.
- Value each person.
- Challenge assumptions.
- Communicate in an open, clear, and honest way.

Our operating principles:

- Give a timely answer and follow through.
- Be approachable, know your role, and really listen.
- Recognize and value our differences.
- Measure success and reward innovation.

Commitment
Employees are expected to:

- Model core values.
- Exceed client expectations.

Our operating principles:
- Make every decision as if you owned the company and were responsible for profit and payroll.
- Identify your customers, know their needs, and deliver as promised.
- Be a role model, set the example, and measure by actions rather than by intentions.

Safety
Employees are expected to:

- Make physical and emotional safety the top priority.
- Protect responsible communication.
- Maintain a drug-free zone.

Our operating principles:

- Safety will not be compromised. We are a "drug-free zone."
- Responsible communication will always be protected.

For each of the six areas above, define how the employee has taken steps to embody your company values. List *specific examples* of times when the employee has either lived up to the values or times when he or she should have done more to meet these expectations.

Overall Performance Rating

This is one of those areas where great minds will agree to disagree. Many leaders argue for a numeric system, while I prefer words. Neither is right or wrong, and the key issue here is that the employee understands where they stand in the organization.

Since I am the author here, the word system wins. Consider the five options — unsatisfactory, marginal, successful, excellent, and outstanding — and their descriptions. Based on the contents of the entire review, choose the one category that most accurately describes the employee's overall performance.

While there are a number of items you could focus on, listed below are some examples of areas to consider:

Technical Skills Required for the Job

Unsatisfactory/ Marginal	Successful	Excellent/ Outstanding
Entry level into the position and/ or entry level into the functional area; lacking in technical skills required for one or more facets of the position; learning curve for job duties is at a slower pace compared to others; difficulty understanding or applying basic concepts of the job; does not continuously improve skills to stay current; skill level less than peers.	Established in job duties; fully competent in technical skills for position; applies technical knowledge in performing most job duties; can explain many technical issues to others; may require additional training in more complex aspects of job; pursues knowledge and appropriate training to stay current in technical aspects of the position.	Has a mastery of skills and expertise and is viewed as a technical expert in job duties; fully competent to train and develop others; applies technical skills to maximize productivity and minimize error; is always current in skills relative to industry.

Communication Skills: Oral, Written, and Customer Relations

Unsatisfactory/ Marginal	Successful	Excellent/ Outstanding
Communication lacks clarity and focus; has difficulty expressing thoughts to others; does not ensure that message has been understood by others; lacks sensitivity in dealing with co-workers and customers; sometimes creates conflict and misunderstanding because of poor communications; does not fully anticipate reactions of others to message; has difficulty listening to and understanding others; interrupts; stifles others; inattentive to input; over elaborates; indirect; fails to inform others; communicates up the line only.	Thoughts are well formulated; determines appropriate method for delivery of messages; communicates to others clearly and concisely; communications to co-workers and customers serve to enhance relationships; can adapt communication style to fit listener; is an active listener; receptive to participation of others in interchange of information; usually provides opportunity for input; projects ease in making presentations; at times may delay presenting news or may be unaware of need to communicate; easy to listen to; listens to others but may overlook input.	Has superb oratory skills and produces highly professional written communications; plans communications proactively to enhance relationships and avoid misunderstanding; displays confidence under stressful speaking conditions; displays ability to maximize customer relations through communication; consistently uses active listening techniques to intensify positive outcomes; consistency tailors presentation style and the presentation to audience; medium captures attention of others; engaging manner; enthusiastic and influential presentation.

Ability to Work Effectively with Others

Unsatisfactory/ Marginal	Successful	Excellent/ Outstanding
Exhibits low energy and interest in becoming involved with others; reluctant to accept responsibility; declines participation on teams unless required; carries less than fair share of workload; sometimes complains about team members; displays impatience, poor timing, or bluntness; lacks personal power; is unable to draw people together or develop networks; lacks consistent success in working effectively in cross-functional teams.	Participates in projects outside of individual goals that will benefit the organization; sometimes encourages working in a coordinated fashion with others to achieve results; is generally willing to become involved; shows interest in team assignments; is a meaningful contributor to the goals of cross-functional teams; builds on the ideas of others; shares information freely; is requested by others to be part of their team; at times may involve too many or too few players; is rarely blinded by personal perspective; may not consistently tap resources wisely but generally perceives how to gain support.	Is excited by the prospect of beginning a project; exhibits high energy and willingness to be involved; solicits others to form a team as a project develops; is asked by others to play a significant role in the team, often as leader; builds relationships across all levels; works with diverse groups effectively; conveys genuine warmth and recognizes the value of individuals; perceives the vantage point of others; adds spark and vigor; uses participating in cross-functional teams as a way to maximize project outcomes.

Here are some suggested categories for overall ratings.

Outstanding

Performance of this caliber is extremely rare and requires that the employee exceed expectations. It is a rating that should be reserved for those who clearly and consistently demonstrate extraordinary and exceptional accomplishments. Those who perform at this level are easily recognized by others outside their own group or division, as well as those in related areas. It is a level of performance that is seldom equaled by others who hold positions of comparable scope and responsibility.

Excellent

This is a rating that best describes a level of accomplishment that goes well beyond a reasonable but demanding standards of performance, especially in the key, critical areas of major responsibilities. This individual consistently demonstrates truly excellent achievement in terms of quality and quantity of output. As an overall rating, this level of performance should describe those who number among the best.

Successful

This rating should be assigned to those whose demonstrated performance clearly meets all the requirements of the position in terms of quality and quantity of output. It describes a solid performance normally expected of those who have the necessary education, training, and relevant experience to enable them to effectively perform in a consistently reliable and professional manner. An employee can still be successful if there are specific developmental requirements.

Marginal

This is a performance that does not fully meet job requirements in all areas of major responsibilities. The individual may demonstrate the ability to complete most assignments; however, the need for further development and improvement is clearly recognized. This individual needs coaching and counseling to achieve a fully competent level of performance.

Unsatisfactory

This is the lowest performance category. It includes the noticeably less-than-acceptable performance of those whose work, in terms of quality and quantity of output, is below minimum job requirements, even when close supervision has been provided. This category describes a level of performance that must significantly improve within a reasonable period if the individual is to remain in the position.

New Employee Assignment

Employee is new to the company and/or the position and the level of contribution cannot be properly appraised because of lack of experience. The focus should be placed on the employee's likely future development.

Here is the form in its entirety:

Section 1 Employee	Title	Department
Date of Hire	Date Completed	Review Period

Position Outcomes — Section 2 (Individual Accountability)
Please briefly describe.

Accomplishments — Section 3 (Individual Accountability)
Please review employee's performance against stated goals and note the impact on the department, group, or company.

1.
2.
3.
4.

Strengths — Section 4 (Growth)

*Please list this individual's top three strengths, and after each, give a **specific example** of an instance where this strength was exemplified. Please include at least one personal strength.*

Strength:

_____
_____
_____

Specific Example:

_____
_____
_____

Strength:

_____
_____
_____

Specific Example:

_____
_____
_____

Strength:

_____
_____
_____

Specific Example:

_____
_____
_____

Barriers to Success — <u>Section 5 (Growth)</u>	
Please list three areas where this individual could improve and exhibit personal and/or professional growth. What do they need to hear rather than what they want to hear?	
	Important/Critical
Area for Improvement:	
Recommendations for Improvement;	
Area for Improvement:	
Recommendations for Improvement;	
Area for Improvement:	
Recommendations for Improvement;	

Employee Personal/Professional Growth Goals and Objectives — Section 6 (Growth)
Please provide an agreed-upon Professional Growth Plan

Employee Comments and Suggestions: How do you feel about the Growth/Trust Development Plan? Do you trust that this process will be used to benefit your growth at GHRO?

Company Core Values — <u>Section 7</u>
Please indicate how well this employee has been modeling the core values and provide specific examples.

Individual Accountability Specific Example:	
Personal Growth Specific Example:	
Integrity Specific Example:	
Respect Specific Example:	
Commitment Specific Example:	
Safety Specific Example:	

Section 8

Overall Performance Rating:

_____

_____

_____

_____

Supervisor's Comments:

_____

_____

_____

_____

_____

_____

_____

_____

_____

	Date
Manager's Signature	
Human Resources Signature	**Date**
Up-One-Level Signature	**Date**
Employee Signature	**Date**

As you can see, in this particular form, the company's core values are woven into the fabric of the review. You may choose another approach; however, I would suggest that this shows the employees that GHRO is serious about its core values and will measure employees on them accordingly.

Face-to-Face Feedback

Okay — form done. Now what? How about the actual conversation with the employee? Effective feedback is critical and more important than any form. Your conversation should be:

- Behavior-based
- Specific
- Objective and job-related
- Fact-oriented
- Constructive and solution-focused
- Clear and quantifiable

Let me give you an example of each, contrasted with a less-effective approach. Consider which of these would have the most meaning to your employee.

Behavior-Based vs. Trait-Based
Behavior-based statement: "Whenever I ask you to do something, you disagree and argue with me in front of other employees."

Trait-based statement: "You have a poor attitude and are hard to get along with."

Specific vs. General
Specific statement: "You are very thorough and attentive to detail, especially in the way you deal with clients. You always get all the necessary information and relay it clearly."

General statement: "You are very thorough in your work."

Objective vs. Subjective

Objective statement: "I have received numerous client comments that your manner is cheerful and pleasant. These are characteristics that are important in our business."

Subjective statement: "You have a great phone manner."

Fact-Oriented vs. Emotionally Charged

Fact-oriented statement: "You rarely, if ever, offer to help others when your work is done; you almost always wait until you're asked. Being viewed as helpful and team-oriented will be important if you wish to make a future with the company."

Emotionally charged statement: "Clearly, you don't care about being part of a team or moving ahead in our organization."

Constructive vs. Accusatory

Constructive statement: "We discussed ways you might get a handle on your anger. One idea is to excuse yourself when a client is making you angry, and then go off and calm down before calling back."

Accusatory statement: "You really messed up this time! You just can't seem to get control of your moods, can you?"

Clear vs. Vague

Clear statement: "It's important you understand the significance of this task. You are proficient in other areas of your job, but failure to meet your sales quota of fifty thousand dollars this month could ultimately cost you your job."

Vague statement: "This is a problem. You had better fix it soon."

The meeting with the employee is very important, particularly to the employee. So remember:

1. **Keep the appointment.** I know you are busy and things come up. I have to warn you however, that changing

appointment dates sends the message to the employee that they are less important than other things you are doing.

2. **Ensure that both you and the employee are prepared.** I have always believed in allowing the employee to write his or her own appraisal. When it is returned to me, I edit it to reflect my thoughts. How better to make sure employees are prepared than having them do some of the work? While some will tell you that employees are harder on themselves than their manager is, I have rarely ever seen this to be true. Given sufficient time, most employees will do a pretty darn good job of writing this document, which of course makes my job a little easier.

3. **Allow sufficient time.** I would not spend more than an hour on any review. Even good feedback has its limits.

4. **Minimize interruptions.** No phone, no e-mail, no Facebook, and please, no Twitter.

5. **Create a nonthreatening atmosphere.** Ideally, this is a positive situation for both you and your employee so keep the mood as light and non -threatening as possible, unless of course you are trying to communicate a very serious message.

You should also provide structure to the meeting.

- **Explain the goals of the meeting.** Are we going over performance, talking about a raise, or setting goals? What is going to happen in the next hour?
- **Encourage a dialogue with the employee.** Ask open-ended questions like:
  - Can you be more specific?
  - Can you give me an example of that?
  - What happened then?
  - How does that affect you?
  - Can you fill me in on the details?
- **Discuss the significant achievements of the employee.** What are some of the great things he or she has done? I cannot emphasize enough the importance of specifics.

People learn from specific feedback and not generalities. Express your own perceptions about the performance — hey, you're the boss, and your opinion counts. Specify the behavior or activity that you want the employee to continue to demonstrate, and verbally express your confidence in the employee's ability to accomplish those goals.

- **Review prior goals.** This is the time to review the goals that were established during the previous review.
- **Discuss areas for improvement.** Review expectations, and make an effort to understand the employee's response by using active listening and reflective questioning techniques. It is not enough to simply tell an employee he or she has a problem. You need to help him or her solve it. It's critically important to provide a timeframe for resolution, otherwise the problem will go on forever. Express your confidence in the employee; this may be difficult in some cases, but honestly, if you can't do this, then skip to Chapter 10.
- **Review future goals and objectives.** Now is the time to look into the future and in collaboration with your employee review future goals and objectives.
- **End on an upbeat note.** When the performance is good this is very easy, however, when the performance is not so good this becomes particularly important. The idea is to help the employee improve their performance and providing encouragement at the end will help achieve this goal.

While your opinion is certainly the most important, there are others who may have an opinion as well. All of the people in the chart below can provide you with valuable feedback on your employee's performance.

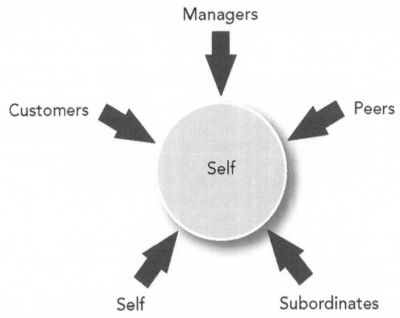

Source: © 2004 The McGraw-Hill Companies, Inc.

Figure 3.1

Finally, on the subject of feedback, there are some common errors in distribution that you will want to avoid: leniency (hey, let's rate everyone well!), strictness (rate everyone poorly — I am a tough grader!), or central tendency (let's rate everyone the same — that way no one can complain!). Errors in distribution pose three problems:

- They make it difficult to distinguish among employees rated by the same person.
- They create problems in comparing the performance of individuals rated by different raters.
- If you use these ratings to distribute raises, you need to be extra diligent about how you finally rate them. In this litigious age, you don't want to end up in court because of how you rate your employees.

You'll also want to avoid the "similar to me" error. I get it — you are great! Unfortunately, your employee is a separate and distinct individual with different and, in some cases, better skills than you have.

That's it. You have established your employees' goals based on organizational goals, written the review, and sat down for that "difficult" discussion. Next, we'll discuss how to pay them.

Chapter 4
How to Make Sure You
Pay Them Correctly

//

Have you heard of the various studies that show that from an employee-satisfaction perspective, pay ranks somewhere between third and fourth. These surveys tell us that employees value their supervisor more than pay, or wanting to have a "say in things." Perhaps this is true, but at the end of the day, when your employee leaves for another job, most of the time more money is involved. So what can you do about it?

One problem with pay is that the term means different things to different people. For some, we are talking about an hourly rate; for others, there may be a bonus involved or even stock options. This chapter will focus on the following issues relative to pay:

- Definition of what pay really is
- What a pay system's objectives should be
- A typical pay model
- Elements of a sound system: internal equity, external equity, and employee equity
- Some different ways to pay people
- Strategic alignment of pay to the business
- The concept of total rewards
- Some thoughts on bonuses

Pay: The What, Why, and How

For our purposes, the definition of pay is as follows: *Pay refers to all types of financial rewards and benefits employees receive as part of their employment with you.*

In the next chapter, we will talk more about benefits and some of the other types of rewards that an employee might consider important. In this chapter, we will limit the discussion to base pay and bonuses.

Beyond the obvious of having to pay someone the minimum wage to keep the government off your back, what are you really trying to achieve with your pay system? I would think at least one or two of the following would apply.

- **Attract and retain employees:** As I suggested earlier, if you are not willing to pay a sufficient wage, you are unlikely to attract the type of talent you need or keep them if they do decide to come onboard. I agree that in this economic environment, finding good people at less money will be possible. However, when things turn around — and they will — can you keep them when other employers start to call?
- **Motivate:** Yes, pay can motivate. While a 1 percent raise is hardly motivating, we have gone through three years of small to no salary increases, so this is an opportunity to use the power of the dollar to motivate your team.
- **Promote skills and knowledge development:** One approach we will talk about is the concept of paying for skills and knowledge rather than just longevity or merit.
- **Shape corporate culture:** How you pay people defines who you are as an organization, as well as provides an ability to shape your culture.
- **Determine and control pay costs:** Of course there are limits to how much we can afford to pay, and a well-defined pay structure will help keep you within those limits.

A typical pay model may look something like this:

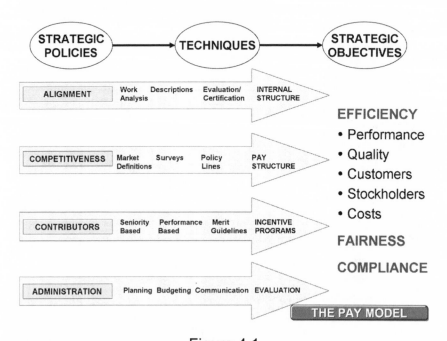

Figure 4.1
Milkovich, G., & Newman, J. (2004). *Compensation* (8th ed.). Boston:
The McGraw-Hill Companies.

This pay model illustrates how an organization can and should align its pay practices to be competitive in order to achieve its strategic objectives.

In Chapter 1, we covered the concepts of alignment. We developed position profiles based on job analysis. The next step in this alignment sequence consists of developing competitive pay practices that meet the test of being:
- Internally equitable;
- Externally equitable; and
- Employee equitable.

Internal Equity

Internal equity is the notion that people should feel that their contribution to the organization, as expressed in pay, is properly proportioned to that of others. For example:

Opinions About Fairness:
Pay Equity

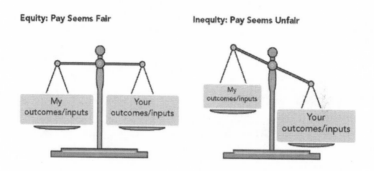

Figure 4.2

Simply put, if I contribute more than you do, I should be paid more. Is it really that simple? Yes, it is — and if you don't believe me, publish everyone's salary, sit in your office, and wait for the feedback. (Just kidding! Please don't do this. But I think you understand where I am going.)

Hopefully, you have analyzed your jobs, written down what people do, and created a position profile. If so, you are ready for the next step, which is to figure out which of these jobs is most important to you.

Now I know you are probably wondering, *What in the world is he talking about? Of course I know what jobs are most important to me.* I have no doubt that you do, and the way you came up with that was probably a simple ranking scheme, which in compensation lingo is called the job evaluation process.

Job evaluation is the process of systematically determining the relative worth of jobs to create a job structure for the organization. This evaluation is based on a combination of job content, skills required, value to the organization, organizational culture, and the external market.

Essentially there are three ways to conduct a job evaluation.

Job Ranking

Raters (usually the owner) look at each job in its entirety and decide which is the most valuable. This is typically what smaller companies do.

Job Classification

Classes or grades are defined to describe a group of jobs. This is a little more complex; it involves setting up a structure ahead of time and putting a job in a certain grade based on its internal value. More on this in a minute.

Point-Factor Method

Numerical values are assigned to specific job components. This means we need to break jobs apart and analyze the smaller parts. We then add up the points to determine the job's worth.

All of these methods have their advantages and disadvantages, as shown below:

	Advantage	*Disadvantage*
Ranking	Fast, simple, easy to explain.	Cumbersome as number of jobs increases. Basis for comparisons not really clear and may appear subjective.
Classification	Can group a wide range of jobs together in one system.	Descriptions may leave too much room for manipulation.

Point	Compensable factors call out basis for comparisons. Compensable factors communicate what is valued.	Can become bureaucratic.

For most small businesses, the ranking system is fine. The most important job — most likely the owner — is ranked highest, and based on whatever criteria make sense, the other jobs fall in line from there.

As organizations grow, however, this becomes more difficult, and you see a move to a classification system. In this system, you group similar jobs together into bands or grades. This is a bit subjective but usually sufficient. At this point, we need to consider what the employees think. As you grow larger employees will look at these grades and wonder how in the heck they were determined. Again, it is about fairness.

For those who really value the idea of internal equity, I would recommend the point-factor method, of which there are a number of good examples available. Under this type of system, you pick a number of important compensable factors and assign points based on the degree of difficulty. For example, one of the universal compensable factors is skill level. Here are some categories that could be assigned points:

- Technical know-how
- Specialized knowledge
- Organizational awareness
- Educational levels
- Specialized training
- Years of experience required
- Interpersonal skills
- Degree of supervisory skills

Effort would be another of these universally compensable factors. Again, examples include:

- Diversity of tasks
- Complexity of tasks
- Creativity of thinking
- Analytical problem-solving
- Physical application of skills
- Degree of assistance available

Responsibility would be the third.

- Decision-making authority
- Scope of the organization under control
- Scope of the organization impacted
- Degree of integration of work with others
- Impact of failure or risk of job
- Ability to perform tasks without supervision

Finally in some cases consider working conditions:

- Potential hazards inherent in job
- Degree of danger that can be spread to others
- Impact of specialized motor or concentration skills
- Degree of discomfort, exposure, or dirtiness in doing job

The next step would be to decide which of these categories carries the most weight and how many points to assign accordingly. You may end up with a chart that looks something like this:

Job Factor	Weight	Degree of Difficulty			
		1	2	3	4
Job Responsibility	50%	100	200	300	400
Education	25%	50	100	150	200

Working Conditions	25%	50	100	150	200

In the category of job responsibility, we assigned a weight of 50% We would assign points from 100 for a low responsibility level to 400 points for the most responsible. Each of these "degrees of factor" would carry a definition so that we are consistent. We would do the same for education, physical effort, and working conditions. When completed, we would have a specific number of points. So what do we do with these points?

Job evaluation points are used to develop salary grades. For example:

Position Title	Job Evaluation Points	Salary Grade	Monthly Pay Range
Senior Administrative Assistant	500	5	$5,000–$6,000
Accountant	450	5	$5,000–$6,000
Secretary	401	4	$4,500–$5,000
Human Resources Assistant	410	4	$4,500–$5,000
Payroll Clerk	325	3	$3,500–$4,500
Account Clerk	320	3	$3,500–$4,500

In this example, Senior Administrative Assistant is placed in a salary grade five and is paid a monthly wage of somewhere between $5,000 and $6,000. Why this amount? Don't worry — we will get there.

The Account clerk, on the other hand, is a salary grade three, which in this system would be the lowest. There is no magic to the number of salary grades, and there are a number of philosophies concerning how best to determine the correct number. My suggestion is to do what makes sense for the organization. Rarely would you need more than ten grades.

External Equity

Once your pay grades are established, you will need to compare them to the market to determine the market rate of the job. This process is known as external equity.

To determine the market value, you will either need to do your own salary survey or use one of the many commercially available products. Let me give you one word of caution: my experience is that you get what you pay for. I have nothing against any free salary survey, but remember that you are making long-term decisions on the basis of this data. I would suggest you invest a little time and money to make sure the data is correct.

What kinds of things should you look at in a salary survey?

- **Key Jobs:** When I refer to *key jobs*, I mean that you don't need to survey every job in the organization. You can take about 25 percent or so of the key ones in each of your salary grades and survey these. In theory, if these 25 percent are in the correct salary grades, then the rest in that grade should be correct as well.

- **Relevant Labor Market:** For most of us, the relevant labor market is our competitors. But do you hire all of your employees from the competition? If so, then yes, this is the correct market. If not, I would look at it geographically. Where do I hire assembly workers? Certainly not nationally. How about in a ten-mile radius? How about managers? Maybe twenty-five to thirty miles?

- **Appropriate Organizations:** In salary surveys, size does most definitely matter. The larger the company, generally the higher the pay. I would concentrate on those organizations that are the closest fit to yours from a sales and number of employee's perspective.

- **The Right Information:** What would you like to know? I would think base pay for sure, but I would also want to know bonus information if available and what salary ranges look like. This is generally expressed as the minimum, midpoint, and maximum of the range. Comparing your ranges to the survey will, on the surface at least, give you some idea if you are competitive.

Once you get this data you need to do something with it.

This chart illustrates individual data points (jobs) and how much they are paid, in this case monthly. This is known as a scatter plot; you can plot the curve as shown below.

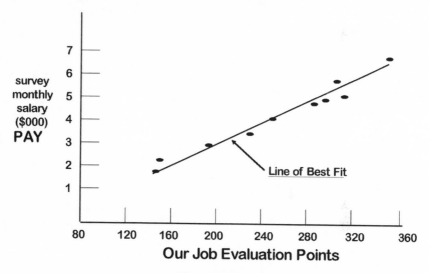

Scatterplot with Linear Curve

Figure 4.3

Milkovich, G., & Newman, J. (2004). *Compensation* (8th ed.). Boston: The McGraw-Hill Companies.

This line represents the "market" and you can then decide how close to the market you wish to pay.

Now, based on what you can afford — and to some extent on the survey information — determine the wages and benefits to be paid. You can design your salary grades with actual dollars like this:

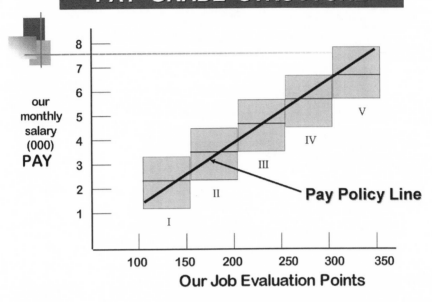

Figure 4.4
Milkovich, G., & Newman, J. (2004). *Compensation* (8th ed.).
Boston: The McGraw-Hill Companies.

Employee Equity

The final consideration should be that of employee equity. Within the grades will be a variation of what employees are paid. How you choose this variation is up to you, but I have always believed in a pay-for-performance system or merit. Here is a quick example:

Minimum	Midpoint	Maximum
$20,000 per year	$30,000 per year	$40,000 per year
Poor performance	Average performance	Great performance
Performance Level #1	Performance Level #2	Performance Level #3

Merit theory would tell you that employees should be paid according to the range that most closely matches their performance. So an average employee should be paid near the midpoint (assuming the midpoint of your range represents the market). A great employee, on the other hand, is paid toward the top of the range; conversely, a poor performer is paid near the minimum. Having said this, let's look at a real life example:

Employee	Pay Rate	Performance Level	How Much Do We Give Them?
Sam	$25,000	2	
Sally	$30,000	3	
Fred	$31,000	1	
Bill	$30,000	2	

In theory, Sam should receive more than Bill, because even though their performance is the same, he is lower in the range. Sally should get the most since she is most out of alignment with her high performance and lower salary. What about Fred? Given his salary and low performance, I would argue we should give him nothing, and I think most of you would agree. The real dilemma is Bill, who is an adequate performer and paid as such. Do we give him more money even though he is properly placed under this model? That is your call, and I am glad I am not making this decision.

These are rarely easy decisions, and don't be surprised if you lose a bit of sleep over them. Of course, you could give everyone the same thing, which leads me to the next subject: What are some of the options of how we can pay people?

There Are a Number of Different Ways to Pay

One of the old sayings in compensation theory is, "You get what you pay for." While this may sound trite, I have to tell you that in thirty years, I have learned firsthand that this is true. Here are some examples of how you can pay people and what you will get as a result.

Standard Rate

In other words, everyone in the same job gets exactly the same amount. But with no incentive to improve or be the best, why bother trying to be the best?

Step Rate

This system is often used in the public sector and looks like this: Each step represents a time period, such as one year. You move up in this system as a function of time, not performance. This is otherwise known as longevity.

Step 1	Step 2	Step 3	Step 4	Step 5	Step 6
$15/hour	$16/hour	$17/hour	$18/hour	$19/hour	$20/hour

Like I said, you get this increase as a function of time on the job, so why bother to improve or be the best?

Piecework

In this system, you are paid by the "piece" or job that is produced. This is literally an example of "You get what you pay for."

Merit

As previously described, people earn different rates within a range based on their performance. Assuming you have measured their performance correctly, as we saw in Chapter 3, then this would seem to incentivize people to do the best job they can.

There are several other systems available, and we could spend multiple chapters on this topic alone, but at the end of the day you need to do what you can afford and what fits your company's culture.

Strategic Alignment to the Business

Whatever pay method you choose needs to closely align to the objectives of the business. One way to think of this is as follows:

Strategic Alignment

VISION/MISSION
CORE BELIEFS
DESIRED CULTURE
BUSINESS OBJECTIVES

REWARD
PLANS

PERFORMANCE

Les Wiletzky

Figure 4.5
Milkovich, G., & Newman, J. (2004). *Compensation* (8th ed.).
Boston: The McGraw-Hill Companies.

Your culture and business objectives define the compensation plan, not the other way around. If things have changed, then change the system. Yes, there will be grumbling and moaning, but for many organizations pay is the highest cost item in their budget, and if you are not aligning it properly to your vision/mission/business objectives, you are missing a tremendous opportunity to impact organizational performance. Here is another look:

Key Steps to Formulate a Compensation Strategy

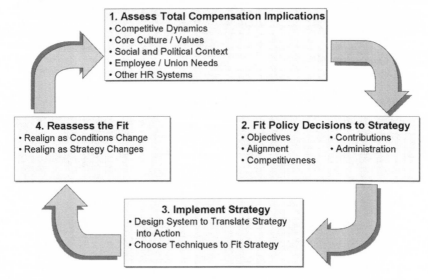

1. Assess Total Compensation Implications
- Competitive Dynamics
- Core Culture / Values
- Social and Political Context
- Employee / Union Needs
- Other HR Systems

4. Reassess the Fit
- Realign as Conditions Change
- Realign as Strategy Changes

2. Fit Policy Decisions to Strategy
- Objectives
- Alignment
- Competitiveness
- Contributions
- Administration

3. Implement Strategy
- Design System to Translate Strategy into Action
- Choose Techniques to Fit Strategy

Figure 4.6
Milkovich, G., & Newman, J. (2004). *Compensation* (8th ed.).
Boston: The McGraw-Hill Companies.

Total Rewards

This chapter is devoted primarily to compensation in its traditional view. We cannot ignore the concept of total rewards, sometimes called total return for work.

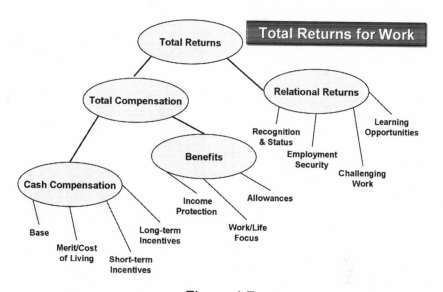

Figure 4.7

Milkovich, G., & Newman, J. (2004). *Compensation* (8th ed.).
Boston: The McGraw-Hill Companies.

Total returns for work looks at your total compensation package and will challenge you to take a holistic approach to compensation. Direct pay generally is 50 to 75 percent of the total compensation picture. What about the other 25 to 50 percent? In Chapter 5, we'll examine the concept of benefits as they fit into the total returns for work model and look at some of the changes Obamacare has brought.

Finally, Some Thoughts on Bonuses

While this is not a book on compensation per se, I thought a discussion in this chapter without a few thoughts on the traditional bonus would be incomplete.

I love a good bonus I really do. There are so many advantages to making a bonus a significant part of an employees pay. For example, if the business suffers a slowdown, you can reduce or eliminate the bonus. Conversely, if you have a great year, let's increase it. Depending upon how the plan is written, if the employee leaves before the bonus is paid, that's it, you don't have to pay it.

To be successful with bonuses, keep in mind a few things:

- **Make sure the plan is clearly communicated.** Nobody likes surprises, particularly when it comes to their money. A bonus is great, but if you don't tell me how to earn it, I have no way of giving you what you are looking for. Remember, you get what you pay for.
- **Make sure the plan is understood.** I hate complexity. I see this so often with sales incentive plans. If the participant doesn't understand the plan, he or she will likely not give you what you are looking for. Again, you get what you pay for — assuming people know *what* you are paying for.
- **Make the bonus easy to calculate.** If you need a PhD in math to calculate the bonus, scrap it. It should be measurable in the simplest way possible. Some people track this information almost daily, others only once in a while.
- **Employees must believe they are being treated fairly.** Even the best bonus will not be accepted if employees believe there is something shady going on. Again, communication is really the key.
- **Pay the bonus as soon as possible after the desired performance.** I believe in paying a bonus no later than thirty days after the results are known. Any later and employees become suspicious.
- **When a substantial portion of pay is tied to performance, the nature of the relationship with the supervisor might change.** When the bonus represents a large portion (15 percent or more) of base pay and one person makes the decision on who gets what, there is a tendency toward silo building and making sure that person providing the bonus is happy as the possible at expense of other employees and the customer.
- **Employees will demand increased sharing of information.** If you tell them the bonus is based on profits, then I guess you will need to share the numbers

concerning profits. While this is kind of obvious, if this doesn't fit your company culture, perhaps another measure is more appropriate.

- **Variable pay-for-performance systems create heightened pressure for performance and cost containment within the organization.** This pressure will come not just from managers, but also from employees themselves. This is often a good thing and should be encouraged. As long as this doesn't interfere with the organization's mission, I don't see any problem.

Chapter 5
How to Select the Proper Benefits Program

//

When I sat down to write this chapter, I felt a cold wave of nausea rush over me. I have been designing benefit plans for companies since 1994, and never have I felt so utterly helpless. As I started to tear up, I realized that Obamacare is and will continue to be a game-changer. Regardless of your political point of view, there is no denying that the next five to ten years will be a pivotal time in the design and administration of employee benefit programs, particularly health insurance. So rather than assigning blame and living in denial, I decided to approach this subject as objectively as I could. I hope I have succeeded.

How Did We Get to This Point?

A look at medical inflation over the last ten years says a lot about the current health care crisis.

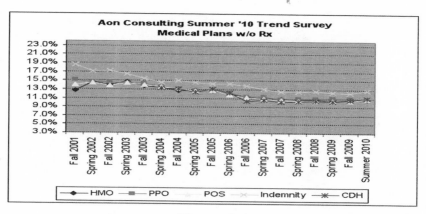

Figure 5.1

I am not an accountant nor am I an economist, but common sense tells me that clearly the inflation in this area is unsustainable. Let's take a quick look at the reasons why.

High Consumer Utilization

Health insurance is much like auto insurance in that the more you use it, the more it costs — and boy, do we use it. As a general rule, for every dollar in premiums sent to the Blue Crosses of the world, patients are to spend eighty cents in claims. The difference allows for the insurance company's costs and profits. But this doesn't explain the year-over-year increases completely.

Behavior is recognized as the primary determinant of health and a major cost driver. I hated to hear that, since I wanted to blame someone else for my insurance costs. As the following chart illustrates, 50 percent of health care costs are behavior-based.

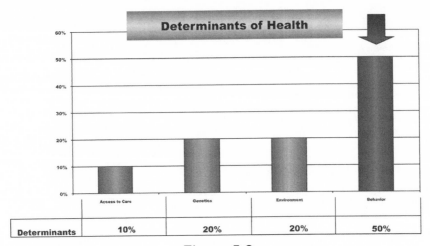

Figure 5.2

Source: IFTF, Centers for Disease Control and Prevention

Prevalence of Preventable Health Conditions
Percentage of Adults

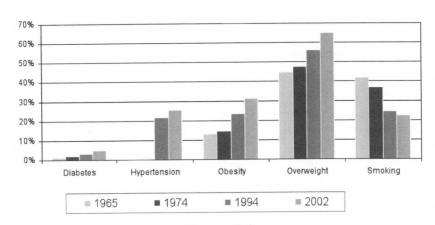

Figure 5.3

Source: Health, United States; CDC National Center for Health Statistics, 2004

We all know what these behaviors are. Overeating, smoking, drinking — you know, all the fun stuff. I remember sharing this with a customer in Minnesota, and thirty minutes into the presentation the employees asked for a break so they could go outside and smoke.

While there are many issues surrounding behavior, no doubt obesity is one of the largest and most costly. We all know obesity is associated with a number of diseases, such as diabetes. Clearly we are not getting any lighter, and this is reflected in our health care costs.

Aging Population

As we age, we require more and costlier health care. The figures are staggering.

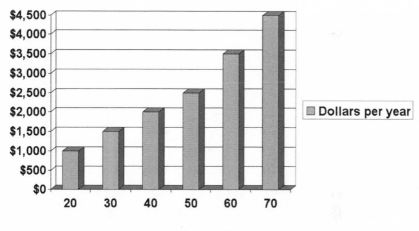

Figure 5.4

High-Cost Technology

The cost of technology, including new and better pharmaceutical products, is causing costs to increase. The fancy drugs you see on TV are just the beginning of a new wave of injectable medication that will make many people's lives easier, but at a tremendous cost.

Unnecessary Care

Although no precise dollar amount can be determined, some authorities contend that insurance fraud constitutes a $100-billion-a-year problem. The United States Government Accountability Office

(GAO) estimates that one out of every seven dollars spent on Medicare is lost to fraud and abuse, and that in 1998 alone, Medicare lost nearly $12 billion to fraudulent or unnecessary claims. Can this really be fixed like Obamacare advocates contend? Who knows?

This is where we are today, and from my perspective, we are entering the great unknown. Unknown is the long-term effect of Obamacare, particularly on small business. Given the proposed health care exchanges due to take affect in 2014, one has to question the wisdom of offering health insurance to your employees in the future. Currently, many of your employees will be entitled to subsidized care, and your cost could actually be less if you allow them to participate.

So what to do? At the end of the day, there are still a number of areas you can address to contain costs. These include:

- **Employee contribution to the premium cost.** Naturally, the easiest way to lower your health-insurance cost is to pass these costs along to the employees. This is a delicate balancing act. I can remember the days when it was normal to pay a fixed percentage of the premium, such as 90 percent of employee and 75 percent of family. These days, this is difficult to do, and I now see more companies moving to a fixed dollar amount for coverage. This is predictable and easier to budget. This approach, however, will require more attention being paid to the other items below.
- **Raising deductibles.** Remember the time when deductibles were $100? Seems like a long time ago. Now we see $500 at a minimum, and $1,500 is more common. The current national average is $1,200. Raising this cost has a huge impact on the premium cost.
- **Change the percentage that the company covers.** Again, not to date myself, but I remember when 100 percent of cost paid by the company was common. This moved to 80 percent, and I am now starting to see 65 percent. One good aspect of Obamacare is the requirement of 100 percent coverage for preventative medicine like physicals,

mammograms, and prostate exams. Now is time for that colonoscopy you have always wanted. A note of caution. Preventative is only preventative if nothing bad is found. If so then the procedure may not be considered preventative and you may need to pay accordingly.

- **Change co-pays.** Co-pays will generally run around twenty dollars for doctor visits. I often wonder, why such a low amount? The average doctor visit is certainly higher than this, so why not fifty dollars?
- **Consider tiering of the drug plan.** A three-tier plan is now common with generic drug, brand, and non-formulary making up the main categories. The best strategy here is to charge the minimal amount possible for generic drugs, thus encouraging your employees to use this less-expensive alternative. Charge more for the other categories, and of course champion the use of mail order prescription plans. These are the least expensive option.
- **Move to a consumerism model.** I believe the future is really in the consumerism model. Let's look at these types of plans in more detail.

Consumerism in Health Care

Consumerism has generally been accepted as a philosophy and/or strategy to move more responsibility and accountability to the health care participant with support from the employer. The premise is that with the right information, resources, and financial involvement, participants will spend dollars more effectively.

The strategies in a consumer-oriented strategy are wide-ranging, from simple cost sharing to a web-enabled health advocates. CDHPs are plan designs and funding vehicles intended to deliver on the promise of consumerism. Before choosing these plans, make sure your company has the necessary elements for such a strategy to work.

Leadership Engagement/Visibility

Senior leadership must be involved and leading the charge. This is not a time for leadership to defer to human resources.

Commitment to Education/Change Management

One of the weaknesses of CDHP is the assumption that employees know how to be health care consumers. Nothing is further from the truth. They need a lot of education and resources to be successful consumers. I like to use the analogy of the evolution of the telephone. Twenty years ago, a telephone was a thing that sat on your wall or desk, and your choices were basically black or white. Today, of course, the cell-phone industry has changed all of this. If your employees can figure out their cell phone, they can certainly become health care consumers. We have been so paternalistic in this area for so long that the change to consumerism will take time.

Longer-Term Employment View

Most CDHPs have a health reimbursement or health savings account attached to them, which implies that employees will stay long enough with the company to take advantage of these tools.

Literate Population

For CDHPs to work, employees need to be literate enough to become consumers. If your organization is composed mostly of low-wage earners who are not particularly literate, I would hesitate to implement this type of plan. Employees will also need to have reasonably good Web access.

Comprehension of Basic Financial Concepts

Like a 401(k), there is some level of financial savvy needed to make a CDHP work. Again, education is the key to success.

Comfort with Shared Benefits Decision Making

This has not been the norm over the past fifty years. Most of these decisions have been made for us by our employers. This needs to change, and your workforce needs to be able to adapt to this.

Some organizations have chosen to only offer a CDHP. This is an aggressive approach; however, it may be the most compelling option because it eliminates selection risk, which enables more accurate design, pricing, and contributions.

A full-replacement CDHP program can include a number of consumer related items, such as:

- Health care advocates who guide the employee through the maze of insurance-company rules and advocate for the employee in getting claims paid and services approved.
- Disease management programs.
- Mandatory Health Risk Assessment (HRA), a very useful tool for identifying health problems before they become chronic. Some companies may compensate employees to participate often adding money to their HRA or HAS
- Prior authorization for certain medications (those most often misused, and over-prescribed and with lower-cost alternatives are targeted).
- Voluntary disease management programs with a health coach.
- Dedicated nurse line for non-emergency concerns.

Other Benefits

Fortunately, there are still areas in the benefit arena that the government has not yet attempted to regulate. Given that you have wide latitude in creating the total benefits package you offer employees, there are a number of other items to consider.

Decisions about which benefits to include should take into account:

- The organization's goals

- The organization's budget
- The expectation of the organization's current employees and those it wishes to recruit in the future

A logical place to begin selecting employee benefits is to establish objectives for the benefits package. When considering these objectives, always bear in mind that your employees' demographics should enter into your decision. For example, while everyone clearly needs health insurance, a twenty-five-year-old may value a pension plan less than a forty-five-year-old. By understanding these differences, you are in a better place to make strategic decisions. These decisions should be made among the following categories of benefits. (Cost and age sensitivity are included. Costs are a relative thing, but by *high* I am referring to hundreds of dollars per employee per month vs. *low*, which would be a few dollars. Age sensitivity refers to the affect of the employee's age on the cost of the benefit.)

Protection Programs	*Cost*	*Age Sensitivity*
Medical Insurance	High	In small groups (fifty or less) there is great sensitivity. In large groups, this is not the case.
Dental Insurance	Medium	In small groups, yes; large groups, no.
Vision Insurance	Low	No
Life Insurance — Term	Low	Yes
Life Insurance — Variable	High	Yes
Short-Term Disability	Low	Yes
Long-Term Disability	Medium	Yes
Paid Time Off		
Vacation	High	No

Holidays	High	No
Sick Time	High	No
Pensions		
Defined Benefit or "Traditional" Plans	High	Yes
Defined Contribution, such as 401(k) or 403(b)	Low unless there is a generous match	No
Voluntary		
Legal Insurance	Low	No
Accident Insurance	Low	No
Dreaded Disease	Medium	No
Long-Term Care	High	Yes
Pet Insurance	Low	No

Your decision to offer any or all of these is based first and foremost on affordability and then next on the needs of your employees. Prices will vary tremendously, and I would always recommend you consult a benefit broker for specific guidance.

Whatever plan you choose needs to include a well thought out communication plan. Organizations must communicate benefits information to employees so they will appreciate the value of their benefits. Communication is essential so that the benefits can achieve their objective of attracting, motivating, and retaining employees.

On the subject of motivation, there are a number of things you can do to motivate your employees that may or may not be considered benefits.

Flexible work schedules have become much more commonplace in the workplace today. With employees able to connect from just about anywhere, the idea of the nine-to-five in the office is simply an outdated concept. Some possible arrangements include:

Flextime

An employee can choose to be in the office at any time, as long as it falls with a predetermined window, such as 10:00 a.m. to 2:00 p.m. Employees can be in the office at any time so long as they are there during these hours.

Compressed Work Week

Many organizations have experimented with four ten-hour days a week, or perhaps a 9/80 where employees work eight nine-hour days with one eight-hour day and every other Friday off. There are many variations on the theme. Before engaging in these changes, please check your local state regulations.

Job Sharing

There may be circumstance when two employees can share one job. Both would, of course, be part-time, which may allow you to save money on benefits. Many employees are looking for this type of flexibility.

Telecommuting

Clearly, in today's environment, employees can work from home, and in many cases be more productive than in the office. Many view this as a "benefit," although not a traditional one. You would have to make sure the home environment is appropriate for this type of arrangement, and there would need to be agreement on the cost of phone, Internet, fax, etc.

The question can be then, what do I offer? What do they want? Are they happy? One potential way to find the answer is to conduct an employee opinion survey. Done anonymously, a survey can be an excellent tool for determining how employees are feeling and what they want. Some areas you should consider surveying include:

- Senior leadership
- Supervision

- The company itself
- The work environment
- Pay and benefits
- Policies and procedures
- The job itself
- Coworkers
- Facilities

Here are some examples of possible statements to ask survey respondents to agree or disagree with:

- There is an environment of openness and trust in my workplace.
- New employees are made to feel welcome when they join the organization.
- Different departments work together to solve problems.

When it is all said and done, employees want to feel valued, and if you accomplish this you have provided the best benefit of all.

Chapter 6
How to Keep Them Safe

//

Employee safety is one of the most important items that you will have to deal with on a day-to-day basis. Not only can this be a huge cost item in the form of workers' compensation, but the morale and health of the workforce is key as well. In this chapter, we will examine the following items:

- Commitment from the top
- What a safety manual should look like
- How to administer the plan with both management and employee responsibilities
- Motivation and counseling
- Communication
- Hazard identification
- Hazard correction and follow up
- Accident investigation
- Training
- Employee safe work practices
- Return to work programs
- Alcohol and drug policies

Commitment from the Top

No safety program will be effective without a commitment from the top of the organization. I would suggest a statement similar to this one:

At the XYZ Company, we are committed to providing a safe, healthy, drug-free and secure work environment for everyone associated with our sites. This commitment goes beyond the very important goal of physical safety and stresses the need for emotional safety as well.

It is our intent to encourage all employees, students, and guests to foster and promote our core value of a safe workplace. This requires the elimination of unsafe acts and conditions. This goal can best be achieved through teamwork between everyone who works in, lives in, or visits our facilities. This also requires your *personal* commitment to ensure that the physical and emotional safety of everyone associated with the XYZ Company is our top priority.

Given this goal, everyone has the responsibility to conduct activities in a safe manner and to immediately correct and/or report unsafe acts or conditions. I expect all of our leaders to implement site-specific measures and create an awareness that will promote safe practices and lead to the achievement of physical and emotional safety for everyone. We are further committed to taking all necessary actions to achieve our goal of zero injuries.

Safety is an integral core value, and I know I can count on your full participation, cooperation, and support in making the XYZ Company a safe and secure place to work, visit and live.

What a Safety Manual Should Look Like

A safety manual is intended to provide everyone in the organization with the information and procedures needed to drive an accident-prevention program. A safety-program coordinator, identified in writing, should be responsible for the implementation and maintenance of your program. Here are some examples of the language you'll want to include in your manual.

- "We are committed to encouraging and motivating employees to comply with the safety rules and safe work practices contained in the safety manual. The repeated failure of an employee to cooperate with safety procedures shall be considered a violation, and they will be referred to human resources for further action."
- "Managers and supervisors are required to see that safety and health information is communicated to all employees. Ideas on the most effective way to communicate are contained in this manual."
- "Injury and illness hazards need to be identified in the workplace. A formal self-inspection program and an equipment evaluation system need to be developed to meet this requirement."
- "Deficiencies or hazards identified during a self-inspection or in an accident investigation must be corrected. The priority attributed to the correction of the hazardous condition should be commensurate with the seriousness of the hazard. Appropriate documentation is necessary."
- "Each work-related injury or illness must be investigated by the employee's immediate supervisor. Forms and procedures for this investigation are included."
- "All employees need to receive training in identifying and guarding against injury hazards associated with their work. The specifics as to how to accomplish the training are also included in this manual."
- "In keeping with our drug-free zone, all locations must have in place a drug testing program that includes pre-hire and post-accident testing."

How to Administer the Plan with Both Management and Employee Responsibilities

Everyone in the company has a role in successfully implementing an accident-prevention plan. Human resources provides overall guidance with respect to program activities and helps insure requirements are met. Individual site safety and security managers are responsible for implementing the program locally. Department managers and supervisors are accountable for the health and safety of their employees. This includes conducting department-specific safety training; supporting the emergency-response plan; enforcing compliance with safety policies and procedures; and adhering to disciplinary procedures. Employees are required to review the Employee Safety Handbook and acknowledge receipt by signature.

The company will need to provide a mechanism for employees to report safety hazards or unsafe acts and conditions. This includes providing resources to:

- Identify and control hazards
- Engineer hazards out of the workplace
- Purchase personal protective equipment (PPE)
- Promote and train employees in health and safety practices

Site managers and supervisors should set a good example as leaders and model our safety core values. This can be accomplished as follows:

- Appropriately wear PPE.
- Respond to and correct workplace hazards or unsafe acts.
- Counsel employees who violate safety policies or safe work practices.
- Promptly respond to employee safety suggestions.

If you have any cleaning supplies, chemicals, spray cans, or other materials that qualify as hazardous, you must maintain a copy of the MSDS (Material Safety Data Sheet) on file for reference in an emergency and for safety training.

While everyone is responsible for safety each person has a specific responsibility.

Individual Employee
- Report work-related accidents immediately.

- Follow all safe work practices and maintenance procedures.
- Report unsafe conditions promptly.
- Participate in safety training on the job.

Supervisor

- Set a positive example by following all safe work practices.
- Enforce all safe work practices.
- Conduct a thorough investigation of any work-related accident, including an interview with the injured worker and a full written description of incident, causation, and corrective actions.
- Arrange for first aid or more advanced medical treatment of injured employee.
- Conduct safety training as needed for new employees and/or new job assignments.

Safety Manager

- Ensure accurate, timely, and thorough evaluation of accident and illness reports.
- Review all accidents within twenty-four hours of receiving accident and illness report from supervisor.
- Assist supervisors and employees in complying with the safety program.
- Ensure that the facility is in compliance with state and federal health and safety regulations.
- Manage the safety program.
- Review and evaluate accident investigation reports.
- Respond and solve safety-related issues involving hazardous operations, air quality, ergonomics, material handling, emergency evacuations, and similar activities.
- Inventory all products considered to be hazardous.
- Maintain a file of MSDSs (Material Safety Data Sheet) for any hazardous materials on site.

- Conduct and/or arrange for employee training on hazard communication, emergency response, and other safety and health subjects.
- Document individual employee safety training.

Human Resources
- Coordinate with any employee properly trained in first aid/CPR to provide first aid, or call emergency services.
- Report all medical and lost time claims immediately to insurance company by phone or fax.
- Communicate with the preferred provider.
- Communicate with and monitor injured worker.
- Verify that all workers' compensation injuries have a supervisor's accident investigation report.
- Maintain the various OSHA logs.
- Ensure communication with insurance adjuster, preferred providers, treating physician, injured worker, rehabilitation, supervisor manager, etc.

While your organization may not be large enough to have all of these funct0ions the responsibilities must be delegated in some fashion to ensure successful implementation of the program.

Motivation and Counseling

A successful safety program needs two elements with respect to employees. I refer to these as the carrot and the stick. In reality, safety can be fun. No, it is really true! A number of my customers utilize programs like Safety Bingo. For every day without an injury, a number is chosen, and when there is a Bingo, the employee gets some kind of prize. If there is an injury, that Bingo card is over and a new one starts the next day. There are many ways to have fun.

The stick has to go along with the carrot. Unfortunately, employees can do very stupid unsafe acts, and there needs to be a consequence to this. For example, I once had an employee — a manager no less — go into a bathroom that was taped off with wet floor signs in prominent display. She was told by the custodian not to enter the bathroom, but guess what? Yup, she went in, slipped, and broke her hip. Fifty thousand dollars in workers' compensation costs later, here we are. Was this an "accident"? I don't believe so, and we disciplined her for breaking obvious safety rules. While you should *never* discipline employees for getting hurt, you can certainly discipline them for not following safety rules.

Communication

One of the keys to implementing a safety program is communication. A method should be in place to communicate both up and down the organization. For example:

- Allow employees an opportunity to voice their concerns about general safety and unsafe acts, conditions, or processes.
- Provide essential and mandatory safety and health training and document attendance.
- Distribute the employee site-specific safety rules to all employees.
- Utilize safety posters, bulletins, newsletters, or similar publications promoting core values.
- The communication system needs to be readily understandable by all employees. You will need to communicate in English and, where appropriate, other languages.

Hazard Identification

Naturally, in order to prevent injuries, you need to identify hazards in the workplace. This generally involves inspections, which should be done on a regular basis. I would recommend a form similar to this.

SELF-INSPECTION CHECKLIST

Name:		Date:	
Loc.:			
"No" Responses Require Correction and Comments			

ADMINISTRATION:	YES	NO	N.A.
1. Are OSHA record-keeping requirements current and properly detailed?			
2. Have *all* accidents been investigated promptly and thoroughly since last inspection?			
3. Are accident-investigation corrective actions being implemented?			
4. Is required and supplemental safety training being scheduled and completed?			
5. Is the MSDS binder current, alphabetized, and complete with an index page?			
Comments:			

EXTERIOR:	YES	NO	N.A.
1. Are parking areas free of large potholes and other defects that could cause trip/fall?			
2. Are exterior lights all in good working order and adequate to light the area?			
3. Are steps, railings, and walkways in good condition, no trip/fall hazards?			
4. Are parking bumpers well secured and clearly visible?			
5. Are personnel gates, fences, and rolling gates working properly and free of defects?			
6. Is the area free of trash or litter?			
7. Other observed hazards?			
Comments:			

OFFICE AREA:	YES	NO	N.A.
1. Are entranceways safely arranged and free of trip hazards?			
2. Are entrance mats or carpets free of tears or corner curls?			
3. Are all exits identified with illuminated exit signs?			
4. Is the emergency lighting system working properly? Actually tested?			
5. Are aisles open and free of trip/fall hazards?			
6. Are aisles and walk areas open and free of materials that block egress?			
7. Are individual work areas free of cords, wires, and other trip hazards?			
8. Are fire extinguishers easily located, tagged, and ready to use?			
9. Is housekeeping in the area up to normal business standards?			
10. Are all electrical outlets provided with the proper cover plates?			
11. Are electric appliances grounded and equipped with three-prong plugs?			
12.Are all electric panels clear and with no exposed wires or circuit breakers?			
13.Is the first-aid kit properly stocked with recommended items?			
14.Are latex gloves, safety glasses, & biohazard labels kept in first aid kit?			
Comments:			
FIRE PROTECTION & PREVENTION	YES	NO	N.A.
1. Are all fire extinguishers properly hung, well identified, and fully charged?			

2. Are monthly visual inspections being made and tags being initialed as required?			
3. Are local fire alarms, smoke alarms, and sprinkler alarms tested as required?			
4. Are at least two smoke detectors actually functioning and tested periodically?			
5. Are the sprinkler riser valves open and protected against tampering?			
6. Are exits clear, properly identified, and well lighted as required?			
7. Are fire/smoke barrier doors kept in a closed position?			
Comments:			

Hazard Correction and Follow-Up

Identifying hazards is one thing, fixing the problems that exist is another. Normally, hazards are prioritized by the severity of the issue. Concerns that could lead to immediate employee injury should be corrected first and the rest prioritized according to severity and cost to correct. There should be a procedure in place to ensure that these hazards are eliminated, and any that remain for the next inspection should receive immediate attention.

Accident Investigation

The purpose of accident investigations is to identify the root cause of the accident to prevent a recurrence. The following is a recommended Accident Investigation Report:

SUPERVISOR'S ACCIDENT INVESTIGATION REPORT

IDENTIFICATION

1. Company or Branch	2. Department	
3. Date of Accident	4. Time AM PM	5. Date Reported
6. Name of Injured	7. Job Title	
8. Experience *(years, months)*	9. Sex □ Male □ Female	
10. Did Accident Occur □ On Premises □ Off Premises	11. Employee Death □ Yes □ No	
12. Person Treating Injury		
13. Did the Injury Result in Lost Time? □ Yes □ No	14. Change in Duties? □ Yes □ No	

INJURY

15. Accident Type
16. Source — the Object or Substance Inflicting Injury
17. Nature of Injury

18. Part of Body

PROPERTY DAMAGE

19. Describe Property, Equipment, or Material Damaged

20. Nature of Damage

21. Source — Object Inflicting Damage

DESCRIPTION *(Describe what happened; who was involved; where; when; why; how.)*

22.

CAUSE *(Identify unsafe acts or conditions; contributory factors; base cause; lack of control)*

23.

137

EVALUATION

24. Severity Potential
☐ Major ☐ Serious ☐ Minor

25. Recurrence Potential
☐ Frequent ☐ Occasional ☐ Rare

26. Have Similar Accident(s) Occurred Before?
☐ Yes ☐ No

27. Reasons for Recurrence

CORRECTION *(Describe steps taken to prevent future accidents)*

28.

FOLLOW-UP *(Pend a copy of the report for follow-up)*

29. ☐ Immediate ☐ 7 Days ☐ 30 Days ☐ 60 Days activity *(List actions taken and dates; estimate cost)*

Supervisor Signature	Date	Employee Signature	Date

138

MATERIAL HANDLING ANALYSIS

1. What was being handled? _____

2. How much did it weigh? _____

3. How high was the lift? _____

4. Did the employee slip while lifting? ☐ Yes ☐ No

5. Did the employee twist while lifting? ☐Yes ☐ No

6. How frequently is it done? _____

7. Were there any abnormal working conditions at the location of the accident (wet floors, material on floors, etc.)? _____

8. How far from the body were the workers' hands at the start of the lift? _____

9. How often is this job done? _____

10. Has the employee had previous injuries or other material-handling injuries? ☐ Yes ☐ No Explain _____

11. Was accident reported immediately? ☐ Yes ☐ No If not, why? _____

12. Who was employee working with at time of accident? _____

This report should be completed within forty-eight hours of the accident and can be used as a training tool in the future.

Training

Training is perhaps the most important element of a safety program. Each employee must receive training relevant to his or her particular job, and records of this training should be kept in a method similar to this one:

EMPLOYEE SAFETY TRAINING RECORD

Date: _____ Location: _____

Presenter: _____

Length of Presentation: _____

OBJECTIVES/OUTLINE:

Employees in Attendance:

1.		11.
2.		12.
3.		13.
4.		14.
5		15.
6.		16.
7.		17.
8.		18.
9.		19.
10.		20

All safety records should be filed for future reference should you ever get visit from OSHA.

Employee Safe-Work Practices

Regardless of your industry, there are basic safe work practices that need to be shared with your employees. Here's a list of guidelines you can distribute and have employees sign off on.

GENERAL SAFETY GUIDELINES

1. It is important that employees report all work-related injuries and illnesses to their immediate supervisor as soon as possible after they become aware of the injury.

2. All employees should exercise extreme care and consideration in the performance of their duties to see they do not cause injury to others or create work hazards that could cause injury to others.

3. All employees shall immediately report any and all unsafe conditions to the safety manager or safety coordinator.

4. No one should try to lift or move heavy or bulky objects, which could cause injury to their backs or other body parts. You are requested to seek assistance from Facilities or from other employees.

5. Personal tools, equipment, extension cords, chemicals, or electrical heaters should not be brought to work without the written permission of management.

6. If it is necessary to use a fire extinguisher, or one has been used without your participation, you should report it to building services as soon as possible so the extinguisher can be recharged or replaced.

7. When you become aware of a defect in a piece of equipment or the building, you should either remove it from service or report it to Building Services so that repairs can be made. Failure to report faulty conditions can result in injuries.

8. When in a hurry, we often create small liquid and food spills. Out of respect for others and to prevent injury that could ensue, all spills should be wiped up immediately rather than left for someone else to remove.

9. Never attempt to repair electrical equipment or appliances. Remove them from service and notify the Facilities Manager to make the proper repairs.

10. Improperly used cabinets can be very dangerous. Opening two drawers simultaneously can cause a file cabinet to crash to the floor. Whenever possible, cabinets should be bolted together in tandem or secured to the wall if it is convenient. Otherwise, training should be given to those who utilize the file-cabinet equipment.

11. Because of the ever-pending possibility of earthquake, heavy objects should be stored on lower shelves while lighter, less dangerous items can be stored on middle and upper shelves.

12. Bookshelves, storage cabinets, and other elevated storage areas should be well secured, bolted to the wall, or unitized in such a way as to reduce tipping in an earthquake.

13. Defective furniture, worn carpets, defective stairs, loose handrails, and other facilities defects that create accident hazards should be reported to Services so repairs can be completed. If possible, remove the object from service.

14. Never run electric cords or cables in walk areas, aisles, or under desks where trip hazards may be created.

15. Report uncovered electric plugs, worn wires, frayed cables, or other electrical hazards to someone who can implement repairs.

16. Everyone should take the time to become educated regarding the emergency procedures in place for responding to fire, earthquakes, or first aid emergencies.

EMPLOYEE DRIVING RULES

1. The Occupational Safety and Health Administration (OSHA) requires that anyone who operates an automobile in the course of employment must wear a seatbelt at all times.

2. Anyone who operates an automobile in the course of employment has the responsibility to drive within the requirements of state law and the motor vehicle code.

3. All employees who drive in the course of their employment are to participate in driver-safety awareness training. This may take the form of classes, video training, written educational materials, and/or safe operating guidelines. Refer to Fleet Safety Manual for requirements.

ERGONOMIC SAFETY GUIDELINES

Those who work at computer workstations for a prolonged period throughout the day should observe the following guidelines for setting up and arranging your work area.

1. Your chair should be adjustable.

2. The chair should be adjusted so that your feet are set firmly on the floor and your upper thighs are parallel with the floor.

3. You should sit up straight, and the main support from the chair should rest firmly against your back and support the lumbar area of your spine.

4. Your monitor screen should be between 18 and 24 inches away from your eyes, and it should be slightly below the horizontal so you look down at the screen at a small angle of about five degrees below the horizontal. The monitor should be centered directly in front of you.

5. If you do word-processing copy work, the material to be copied should be hung adjacent to the screen so that neck and eye movement is minimized.

6. Lighting should be arranged so there is minimal glare on the screen. For those working near windows, glare screens may be advisable.

7. Keyboards should be located in such a way as to minimize arm and wrist strain. Consult the Human Resources department for additional information.

TEN BASIC ERGONOMIC TIPS

1. Review proper workstation setup and evaluate your workstation in comparison to guidelines and explanations of proper set-up strategy.

2. Remember to set your chair first and then adjust your keyboard height. We advise a slight negative tilt in the tray to keep a full neutral position in the wrist.

3. Take frequent short breaks from the computer by mixing your work duties and performing other work tasks.

4. Discipline yourself to begin mouse work left- and right-handed. Start slow at first and complete the process of sharing 50-50 over a period of about two months.

5. Set up your desk to minimize excessive reaching.

6. Always use a headset if you work on the phone while using the computer for two or more hours per day.

7. Do not use wrist braces and other devices without a doctor's advice.

8. Report pain and discomfort early so steps can be taken to resolve problems and suggest remedies.

9. If you are working in discomfort and/or want assistance evaluating your workstation, ask Human Resources for help.

I have received, read, and understand the safe work practices of my department. I also understand that as part of our core values, I am obliged to follow them in my work activities. Supervisors and the Safety department will have job-specific safe-work practices in addition to these rules.

Date _____   Signature _____

_____ Print Name _____

Date _____Supervisor's Signature _____
                              Print Name_____

Return-to-Work Programs

Research has shown that employees who are able to return to work even with modified duty are quicker to heal than those who sit at home watching attorney ads on the television. In addition, early return-to-work programs contain workers' compensation costs, provide assistance to injured employees while they are recovering, and promote a strong communication system between all parties.

For a return-to-work program to be successful, the following steps must be completed:

1. Obtain commitment and support from site management for the implementation of the early return-to-work program.
2. Appoint a return-to-work manager or coordinator knowledgeable in both workers' compensation and personnel issues to be the coordinator of the program.
3. Establish a policy statement.
4. Identify certain positions that can serve as transitional jobs.
5. Develop written job descriptions for all jobs, including the transitional jobs within your organization.
6. 6Establish procedures for placement of workers into transitional jobs. Limit the number of positions, and place a time limit on the amount of time an injured employee may work in a transitional position.
7. Identify industrial medical clinics near each of your facilities that are experienced in handling industrial injuries. If you are not familiar with any medical providers near your facilities, contact your claims examiner.
8. Identify a primary contact at the clinic.
9. The physician and other clinic personnel should tour the worksite at least annually.
10. Send the industrial medical clinic a letter introducing early return-to-work.
11. Provide the medical providers with up-to-date job analysis.

12. Inform your employees, supervisors, managers, unions, and medical provider(s) that the company will, when possible, accommodate work restrictions by assigning the injured worker to a transitional position.

13. Following each lost-time injury, send the doctor/clinic a medical referral/work status form and note that your company will provide transitional work.

14. 1Communicate with your employees following an injury.

15. Maintain ongoing communication with your claims examiner. Report to the claims examiner as soon as employee returns to work. Provide the claims examiner with copies of all correspondence to the clinic regarding return to work.

16. 1Communicate with your employees who are missing time from work and working in transitional jobs. Maintain a log of your communication with employees.

17. Implement the early return-to-work program consistently. Procedures and time limits should be followed in every lost-time case.

Alcohol and Drug Policies

Drug testing has proven effective in reducing injuries and lowering workers' compensation claims. This is particularly true of post-accident drug testing in which you test employees after an accident or incident. States have different rules, so I would encourage you to check with your attorney or HR consultant before implementing a policy. Here is what a policy might look like.

I. Purpose of Policy

The following written policy ("Policy") is intended to serve as XYZ Company's (hereinafter referred to as "Company") written drug-testing policy. This Policy is intended to be provided and distributed to all affected employees upon adoption of this Policy, to a previously unaffected employee upon transfer to an affected position under this Policy, and to all job applicants upon hire and before any testing of the applicant if the job offer is made contingent on the applicant passing a drug test.

This Policy shall also be available for inspection in Company's Human Resources office during regular business hours, and may be inspected by Company employees or applicants.

It is the intent of the Company to maintain a workplace that is free of drugs and alcohol and to discourage drug and alcohol abuse by its employees. This is one of our core values, and employees who are under the influence of drugs or alcohol on the job compromise the Company's interests and endanger their own health and safety and the health and safety of others. Substance abuse in the workplace can also cause a number of other work-related problems, including absenteeism and tardiness, substandard job performance, increased workloads for co-workers, behavior that disrupts other employees, disruption of customer relations, and inferior quality in services rendered.

To further its interest in avoiding accidents, to promote and maintain safe and efficient working conditions for its employees, and to protect its business, property, equipment, and operations, the Company has established this Policy concerning the use of alcohol and drugs. Each employee is expected to abide by the terms and conditions as set forth in this Policy.

II. Definitions

For the purposes of this Policy:

(1) "Confirmatory test" and "confirmatory retest" means a drug or alcohol test conducted pursuant to a method of analysis allowed under this Policy pursuant to Section IV-B, below.

(2) "Illegal drug" means any drug or substance that (a) is not legally obtainable; or (b) is legally obtainable but has not been legally obtained; or (c) has been legally obtained but is being sold or distributed unlawfully; or (d) to the extent not already set forth in subsections (a)-(c), any controlled substance as set forth in Minn. Stat. § 152.02.

(3) "Legal drug" means any drug, including any prescription drug or over-the-counter drug, that has been legally obtained and that is not unlawfully sold or distributed.

(4) "Drug testing" or "drug test" means analysis of a body component sample according to the procedures set forth under Section IV-B of this Policy, for the purpose of measuring the presence or absence of drugs, alcohol, or their metabolites in the sample.

(5) "Safety-sensitive position" means a job, including any supervisory or management position, in which an impairment caused by drug or alcohol usage would threaten the health or safety of any person.

(6) "Abuse of any legal drug" means the use of any legal drug (a) for any purpose other than the purpose for which it was prescribed or manufactured; or (b) in a quantity, frequency, or manner that is contrary to the instructions or recommendations of the prescribing physician or manufacturer.

(7) "Reasonable suspicion" includes a suspicion that is based on specific personal observations, such as an employee's manner, disposition, muscular movement, appearance, behavior, speech or breath odor; information provided to management by an employee, by law enforcement officials, by a security service, or by other persons believed to be reliable; or a suspicion that is based on other surrounding circumstances.

(8) "Possession" means that an employee has the substance on his or her person or otherwise under his or her control.

III. Prohibited Conduct
A. Scope
The prohibitions of this section apply whenever the interests of the Company may be adversely affected, including any time the employee is:

(1) On Company premises;

(2) Conducting or performing Company business, regardless of location;

(3) Operating or responsible for the operation, custody, or care of Company equipment or other property; or

(4) Responsible for the safety of others in connection with, or while performing, Company-related business.

B. Alcohol
The following acts are prohibited and subject an employee to discipline: under Section V, below:

(1) The unauthorized use, possession, purchase, sale, manufacture, distribution, transportation, or dispensation of alcohol; or

(2) Being under the influence of alcohol.

C. Illegal Drugs
The following acts are prohibited and subject an employee to discipline under Section V, below:

(1) The use, possession, purchase, sale, manufacture, distribution, transportation, or dispensation of any illegal drug or other controlled substance; or

(2) Being under the influence of any illegal drug, or other controlled substance.

D. Legal Drugs
The following acts are prohibited and subject an employee to discipline under Section V, below:

(1) The abuse of any legal drug;

(2) The purchase, sale, manufacture, distribution, transportation, dispensation, or possession of any legal prescription drug in a manner inconsistent with law; or

(3) Working while impaired by the use of a legal drug whenever such impairment might:

(a)   Endanger the safety of the employee or some other person;

(b)   Pose a risk of significant damage to Company property or equipment; or

(c)   Substantially interfere with the employee's job performance or the efficient operation of the Company's business or equipment.

IV. Drug and Alcohol Testing

A.   Persons Subject to Testing

The following individuals are and will be subject to Company's drug testing procedures as set forth in this written Policy:

(1)   Applicants
As part of the Company's employment screening process, any applicant to whom an offer of employment is made must pass a test for controlled substances, under the procedures described in Section IV-B below. The offer of employment is conditioned on a negative test result. The Company will not withdraw any offer of employment on the basis of a positive test result from an initial screening test unless and until that initial test has been verified by a confirmatory test.

If an applicant refuses to cooperate with the administration of the drug test, the refusal will be handled in the same manner as a positive test result.

(2) Employees upon Reasonable Suspicion

The Company's site director or Human Resources manager may order an employee to undergo drug testing under the following circumstances:

(a) If the Company's site director or Human Resources manager has a reasonable suspicion that the employee is under the influence of drugs and/or alcohol;

(b) If the Company's site director or Human Resources manager has a reasonable suspicion that the employee has violated the employer's written work rules as set forth in this Policy prohibiting use, sale, transfer, or possession of drugs while working or on the Company's premises;

(c) If the Company's site director or Human Resources manager has a reasonable suspicion that the employee has sustained personal injury or has caused another employee to sustain personal injury; or

(d) If the Company's site director or Human Resources manager has a reasonable suspicion that the employee has caused a work-related accident or was operating or helping to operate machinery, equipment, or vehicles involved in a work-related accident. All work-related accidents will result in a drug test as specified in this policy.

If an employee refuses to cooperate with the administration of the drug test, the refusal will be handled in the same manner as a positive test result.

(3)   Employees Involved in Treatment Program

Where an employee has been referred by the Company for chemical dependency treatment or evaluation or is participating in a chemical dependency treatment program under an employee benefit plan, the Company may request or require an employee to undergo drug and alcohol testing without prior notice during the evaluation or treatment period and for a period of up to two years following completion of said prescribed chemical dependency treatment program.

If an employee refuses to cooperate with the administration of the drug test, the refusal will be handled in the same manner as a positive test result.

(4)   Employees in Safety-Sensitive Positions

The Company reserves the right to request or require any employee who occupies a safety-sensitive position to undergo drug testing on a random selection basis. Said random selection basis is pursuant to a scientifically valid method.

If an employee refuses to cooperate with the administration of the drug test, the refusal will be handled in the same manner as a positive test result.

(5)   Employees as Part of Routine Physical Exam

The Company reserves the right to request or require an employee to undergo drug testing as part of a routine physical examination. In no event may the Company request or require a drug test in conjunction with a physical examination more than once annually. Whenever the Company requests or requires an employee to undergo drug testing as part of a routine physical examination, the employee will be given at least two weeks' written notice that a drug test may be requested or required as part of the physical examination.

If an employee refuses to cooperate with the administration of the drug test, the refusal will be handled in the same manner as a positive test result.

B. Procedures for Drug and Alcohol Testing

Before requesting an employee or applicant to undergo drug testing, the Company shall provide the employee or applicant with a form that shall (a) confirm that the employee or applicant has seen the Company's written drug-testing Policy, and (b) allow the employee or applicant to disclose any over-the-counter or prescription medications that the individual is currently taking or has recently taken and any other information relevant to the reliability of, or explanation for, a positive test result.

The Company will refer the applicant or employee to an independent, National Institute on Drug Abuse (NIDA)-certified medical clinic or laboratory, which will administer the test for the presence of alcohol, drugs, or other controlled substances. The Company will pay the cost of the test and reasonable transportation costs to the testing facility. The employee will have the opportunity to alert the clinic or laboratory Human Resources to any prescription or nonprescription drugs that he or she has taken that may affect the outcome of the test. All testing will be performed by urinalysis.

The clinic or laboratory, within three (3) working days of a negative test result or positive confirmatory test result, shall disclose to the Company the written test result report for each sample tested. The Company, in turn, shall, within three (3) working days after receipt of a test result report from the testing laboratory, inform in writing an employee or applicant who has undergone drug testing of (a) a negative test result on an initial screening test or of a negative or positive test result on a confirmatory test, and (b) the right provided in Minnesota Statutes § 181.953(8) (see section IV-G, below), which sets forth an employee or applicant's right to request and receive from the Company a copy of the test result report on any drug test. If an employee fails the test, he or she will be considered to be in violation of this Policy and will be subject to discipline accordingly.

C.   **Right to Test Result and Right to Confirmatory Retest**

Pursuant to Minnesota statute § 181.953(8), an employee or applicant has the right to request and receive from the employer a copy of the test result report on any drug or alcohol test.

An employee or applicant may also request a confirmatory retest of the original sample at the employee's or applicant's own expense after notice of a positive test result on a confirmatory test. An employee or applicant who so elects must, within five (5) working days after notice of the confirmatory test result, notify the employer in writing of his or her intent to obtain a confirmatory retest. If the confirmatory retest does not confirm the original positive test result, no adverse Human Resources action or discipline will be taken against the employee or applicant.

D.   **Acknowledgment and Consent**
Any employee subject to testing under

this policy will be asked to sign a form acknowledging the procedures governing testing, and consenting to (1) the collection of a urine sample, hair sample, or other sample for the purpose of determining the presence of alcohol or drugs, and (2) the release to the Company of medical information regarding the test results. Refusal to sign the agreement and consent form, or to submit to the alcohol and/ or drug test, will result in the revocation of an applicant's job offer or will subject an existing employee to discipline up to and including termination.

E.   Confidentiality
All alcohol and/or drug testing-records will be treated as confidential.

V.   Disciplinary Action

A.   Employee Actions Subject to Discipline

Whenever an employee engages in prohibited conduct as defined in Section III-A through III-D above, the employee will be subject to discipline under this section if the employee's actions:

(1)   Caused injury to the employee or any other person, or, in the sole opinion of management, endangered the safety of the employee or any other person;

(2)   Resulted in significant damage to Company property or equipment, or, in the sole opinion of management, posed a risk of significant damage;

(3)   Involved the sale or manufacture
        of illegal drugs or other controlled
        substances;

(4)   Involved the use, possession,
        distribution, or dispensation of illegal
        drugs or other controlled substances;

(5)   Involved an employee under the
        influence of alcohol or the unauthorized
        use, possession, purchase, sale,
        manufacture, distribution, transportation,
        or dispensation of alcohol;

(6)   Involved the failure of an employee to
        report a criminal conviction, as required
        by Section VIII below.

B.   Effect of Violation of Policy

Where the employee has engaged in prohibited
conduct as defined in Section III A-D above,
the employee will be immediately subject to
discharge.

C.   Positive Confirmatory Drug Test Subjects
Employee to Discipline

Where any employee under Section IV-A
(2) - (5) undergoes a drug test pursuant to
the procedures outlined in this written Policy,
and such test yields a positive result from an
initial screening, the Company shall not take
any adverse action against the employee
until the results are verified by a confirmatory
test. Where the positive initial test is verified

by a confirmatory test, the employee shall be subject to discipline pursuant to Section IV-B, above.

Any employee may request a confirmatory retest of the original sample at the employee's own expense after notice of a positive test result on a confirmatory test. Any such request must be in writing and received by the employer within five (5) working days after notice of the confirmatory test result.

All employees have the right to request and receive from the Company a copy of the test result report on any drug test.

D. **Positive Confirmatory Test Subjects Applicant to Withdrawal of Offer**

Where any applicant under Section III-A (1) undergoes a drug test pursuant to the procedures outlined in this written Policy, and such test yields a positive result from an initial screening, the Company shall not withdraw any offer based on a positive test result from the initial screening test until the results have been verified by a confirmatory test. Where the positive initial test is verified by a confirmatory test, the Company reserves the right to withdraw any offer previously extended.

E. **Effect of Discharge on Eligibility for Rehire**

Employees who are discharged for a violation of this Policy will not be eligible for rehire by the Company.

VI. Employee/Applicant's Right to Explain Positive Test Result

Where any employee or applicant under Section III-A (1)–(5) has undergone drug testing which has yielded a positive confirmatory test result, the employee shall have the right, within three (3) working days after notice of a positive test result on a confirmatory test, to submit information to the employer to explain that result, or may request a confirmatory retest of the original sample at the employee's or job applicant's own expense as provided under Minnesota Statutes § 181.953, subdivision 9.

No other appeal procedures are permitted under this Policy.

VII. Management Awareness

Managers and supervisors should be attentive to the performance and conduct of those who work with them and should not permit an employee to work in an impaired condition or to otherwise engage in conduct that violates this Policy. When management has reasonable suspicion to believe that an employee or employees are working in violation of this Policy, prompt action will be taken to address the violation.

VIII. Criminal Convictions

Employees must notify the Company of any conviction under a criminal drug statute for a violation occurring in the workplace or during any Company-related activity or event. Employees must notify the Company within five days after any such conviction.

IX. Use of Legal Drugs

The Company recognizes that employees may, from time to time, be prescribed legal drugs that, when taken as prescribed or according to the manufacturer's instructions, may result in impairment. Employees may not work while impaired by the use of legal drugs if the impairment might endanger the employee or someone else, pose a risk of significant damage to Company property, or substantially interfere with the employee's job performance. If an employee is so impaired by the appropriate use of legal drugs, he or she should not report to work, but must contact his/her supervisor to report the absence as set forth in this handbook. To accommodate the absence, the employee may use accrued sick leave or vacation time. The employee may also contact Human Resources manager to determine whether or not he or she qualifies for an unpaid leave of absence, such as family care or medical leave. Nothing in this Policy is intended to sanction the use of accrued sick leave or vacation time to accommodate absences due to the abuse of legal drugs. Further, nothing in this Policy is intended to diminish the Company's commitment to employ and reasonably accommodate qualified disabled individuals. The Company will reasonably accommodate qualified disabled employees who must take legal drugs because of their disability and who, because of their appropriate use of such drugs, cannot perform the essential functions of their positions adequately or safely.

X. Unregulated or Authorized Conduct

A. Customary Use of Over-the-Counter Drugs
Nothing in this Policy is intended to prohibit the customary and ordinary purchase, sale, use, possession, or dispensation of over-the-counter drugs, so long as that activity does not violate any law or result in an employee being impaired by the use of such drugs in violation of this Policy.

B. Authorized Use of Alcohol
The Company may provide alcohol for consumption at certain events, such as social functions. The consumption of alcohol at these events does not violate this policy.

XI. Confidentiality

Disclosures made by employees to the Human Resources manager concerning their use of legal drugs will be treated confidentially and will not be revealed to managers or supervisors unless there is an important work-related reason to do so in order to determine whether it is advisable for the employee to continue working. Disclosures made by employees to the Human Resources manager concerning their participation in any drug or alcohol-rehabilitation program will be treated confidentially.

XII. Counseling/Rehabilitation

The Company maintains an employee-assistance program that provides help to employees who seek assistance for drug or alcohol abuse, as well as for other personal or emotional problems. Employees who suspect that they may have alcohol or drug problems, even in the early stages, are encouraged to voluntarily seek diagnosis and to follow through with the treatment as prescribed by qualified professionals. Employees should be aware that participation in the employee-assistance program will not necessarily shield them from disciplinary action for a violation of this Policy, particularly if discipline is imposed for a violation occurring before the employee seeks assistance.

XIII.   Counsel

Contact the V.P., Human Resources and Administration, at XYZ Company for counsel and/or interpretation of this policy.

Written Drug Testing Policy
Acknowledgement Form

I, the undersigned, understand that, in pursuit of its goal of a drug-free workplace, I have been requested by XYZ Company to undergo a drug test pursuant to XYZ Company's written drug-testing policy. I hereby acknowledge that I have seen and read XYZ Company's written drug-testing policy and have been granted an opportunity to ask questions in conjunction therewith. I also understand that my failure or refusal to cooperate with the administration of a drug or alcohol test under XYZ Company's written drug-testing policy will be construed in the same manner as a positive test result.

In the box provided below on this form, I have indicated any over-the-counter or prescription medications I am currently taking or have recently taken. Further, I have provided any and all other information, which may affect the reliability or veracity of the test results.

PLEASE LIST ANY PRESCRIPTIONS OR OVER-THE-COUNTER MEDICATIONS YOU ARE CURRENTLY TAKING, ALONG WITH ANY OTHER INFORMATION YOU BELIEVE MAY AFFECT THE RELIABILITY OF THE TEST

Dated:_____

Keeping your employees safe is not only the right thing to do for the business but is also simply the right thing to do. The area of safety can be very technical and I would always advise getting further advice from your human resources or safety professional.

Chapter 7
How to Deal with Their Issues

//

Let's face it — everyone has issues. Rarely a day goes by that I don't spend some time on a problem between an employee and his or her boss, subordinate, or peer. The real trick is understanding which of these is just normal griping and complaining and which is real and requires action. Unfortunately, there is no real way to know until you investigate further. As a result, treat every complaint seriously. While John may be one of those "complainers," at some point he may actually have a real issue, and if you didn't take it seriously … well, see Chapter 8.

I would also set up a procedure that allows employees to keep their grievances internal rather than take them to an outside source, such as the Equal Employment Opportunity Commission or equivalent state agency. I would suggest a dispute-resolution process similar to this one.

DISPUTE RESOLUTION AND ARBITRATION POLICY

Application:
This policy is applicable to XXXX Corporation (the Company) and its employees. Where bargaining units exist, please refer to the applicable labor agreement.

Purpose:

The purpose of this policy is to provide employees with a fair and equitable dispute-resolution procedure that is consistent with the Company's core values, and to preserve the Company's relationship with its employees. This policy is intended to encourage people to sit down, talk, and listen to each other. The ultimate goal is to have everyone agree on a course of action that is fair and equitable to all parties. However, in the event that we are unable to agree on a resolution, both the Company and the employee are required to resolve their disputes through the binding-arbitration procedure set forth below.

Policy:

The Company is committed to the principle that all employees and the Company have the right to a fair resolution of their issues and concerns. Consistent with the Company's core values, all issues and concerns will be resolved in a timely manner as set forth in this procedure. Employees who utilize or who participate in this policy will not be subject to any form of retaliation for doing so. However, employees will be responsible for following established policies and practices while their issues and concerns, and those of the Company, are being addressed. The intent of this policy is to allow employees and the Company to bring forth disputes between themselves, their supervisors, and/or their peers. These include disputes concerning performance reviews, disciplinary issues (including termination), failure to comply with any of the rules and regulations set forth in the employee handbook or required by custom and practice in our workplace, and other issues concerning the workplace. Notwithstanding this formal and required dispute resolution procedure, there are many issues (such as policy interpretations and changes in work responsibilities) that can and should be resolved through informal discussions with site management and, where necessary, the corporate office.

Definitions:

The core values are the guiding principles that apply to all employee actions

The company has established the following five resolution opportunities to address any issue/problem that cannot first be resolved informally by the employee and his/her supervisor.

Level 1 Resolution Opportunity: Employee, employee's supervisor, department head, and Human Resources.

Level 2 Resolution Opportunity: Peer-review committee and recommendation to the site director. A peer-review committee will have three members, including one permanent member and two rotating members. The peer-review committee members will receive appropriate training and be selected by the site senior-leadership team.

Level 3 Resolution Opportunity: Site-director review.

Level 4 Resolution Opportunity: Mediation. In mediation, a professionally trained mediator helps the parties work out their own mutually agreeable solution to the dispute. The mediator will not decide who is right or wrong, nor will he or she render a decision of any kind.

Level 5 Resolution Opportunity: Binding arbitration. This is a process in which a disagreement between two or more parties is resolved by an impartial individual, called an arbitrator, in order to avoid costly and lengthy litigation.

Procedure:

The first step in any issue-resolution process involves open and honest communication between the employee and his or her supervisor. In most cases, this will result in a mutually agreeable solution. Issues that are not resolved in this manner will be subject to the following dispute-resolution procedure:

Level 1: The employee or the Company will make a written request to Human Resources within ten working days of the events giving rise to the dispute, requesting a meeting between the employee, employee's supervisor, department head, and a representative from Human Resources. This meeting will normally take place within ten working days of the written request. Should all parties not be available, this time frame will be extended. A proposed resolution of the dispute will be given by the employee's supervisor and department head to the head of Human Resources and the employee in writing within ten working days of the meeting. If the parties agree to the proposed resolution, the case is closed.

Level 2: If no mutual agreement is reached at Level 1, the Company or the employee shall request a hearing before the local site peer-review committee. The request for a hearing must be made in writing to Human Resources or the employee within ten working days of the conclusion of the Level 1 proceedings. This hearing will take place within ten working days of the written request. Should all parties not be available, this time frame will be extended. The peer-review committee will make a written recommendation to the site director and the employee within ten working days of the hearing. If the parties agree with the written recommendation, the case is closed.

Level 3: If no mutual agreement is reached at Level 2,

the employee or the Company may request a review by the site director. The request for review by the site director must be made in writing to the site director or the employee within ten working days of the conclusion of the Level 2 proceedings. The site director will meet with the employee and a representative of the Human Resources department within ten working days of receipt of the written request and will render a decision in writing within ten working days after the meeting. Should all parties not be available, this time frame will be extended. If mutual agreement is reached, the case is closed.

Level 4: If no mutual agreement is reached at Level 3, either the employee or the Company may request the services of an outside mediator. The request for mediation must be made in writing to the vice president of Human Resources and Administration or the employee within ten working days of the conclusion of the Level 3 proceedings, The Company shall pay the reasonable fees of the mediator and the expenses associated with the mediation. The parties shall mutually select a mediator from some recognized mediation service, such as ADR Services, Inc., ARC, or any arbitration panel established by a court in the state in which the employee works, to select the mediator and conduct the mediation. The vice president of Human Resources and Administration shall facilitate a meeting between the mediator, site representatives, and the employee. The employee may bring anyone to this meeting who can help with the resolution process. This meeting will take place as quickly as possible given the schedules of all sides. Employees will not be paid for time they miss from work to participate in the mediation proceedings. If mutual agreement is reached, the case is closed.

Level 5: If no mutual agreement is reached at Level 4 or if either party wishes to pursue statutory or common-law claims against the other, the employee and the Company will be subject to binding arbitration as provided in the attached arbitration policy and acknowledgment. The party seeking arbitration shall file a written demand for arbitration with the American Arbitration Association and serve a copy on the other party within thirty days after the conclusion of the Level 4 proceedings, except that in any matter involving a statutory or common-law claim, the demand for arbitration must be filed and served no later than the expiration of the statute of limitations applicable to the claim at issue. The vice president of Human Resources and Administration or designee and the employee shall mutually select a neutral arbitrator to hear the case, and the parties will arrange for the services of the arbitrator. The employee will be responsible for the arbitrator's fee and that of the American Arbitration Association up to the amount that the employee would be required to pay to file the same claim in state court. The Company will pay the balance of the fees of the arbitrator and the American Arbitration Association, subject to the power of the arbitrator to award such fees and costs as part of the ruling on the claim. The arbitrator's decision is final and binding, and there is no further appeal other than as provided for in the arbitration policy set forth below. The final award shall be enforceable as provided under applicable federal law or the law of the state in which the employee works regarding the enforcement of arbitration awards.

Forms:
Dispute Resolution Form

Counsel:
The vice president of Human Resources and Administration is responsible for the interpretation of this policy.

Dispute resolution allows employees to air their grievances in a safe forum and resolve the problem or dispute internally. I have typically used this process to resolve disciplinary actions and disagreements concerning performance reviews and work assignments. Peer-review-committee training is provided, and it is interesting to watch these committees at work. They take their job very seriously, and it can be very powerful to hear feedback from your peers as opposed to your supervisor.

There are some disputes, of course, that do not lend themselves to this process. Sexual harassment, discrimination, and anything very confidential in nature may not fit this process.

Let's go back to that complaining employee. Every complaint, no matter how silly on the surface, needs to be investigated. Therefore, it is important to have someone in your organization trained to conduct investigations. Here are the key steps that should be considered.

1. Your initial meeting should be with the employee raising the complaint. Be sure that the employee is comfortable with you handling the investigation.
2. Get the facts — who, what, when, where, how and why. Start with very general open-ended questions, moving to a discussion of facts and finally getting to the details.
3. Determine if an internal investigation is sufficient, or if the issue is large enough to bring in an outsider, such as an HR consultant, professional investigator or attorney.
4. Will a single answer resolve the complaint? Normally this is the case, but sometimes the issues are more complex.
5. Are other employees involved? If so, who are they and do they need to be interviewed? I would normally limit the scope of the investigation to the extent possible, but it is important to get all of the facts, which may involve interviewing a number of people.
6. Do you need more facts than the employee is able to provide? If so, try to determine where these facts might reside.
7. Do you need the help of any other resource in order to reach a conclusion? If so, go get them.

8. Interview the complainant in person as soon as possible. The goal is to identify all issues and concerns, no matter how egregious. Advise them of the anti-retaliation policy and against speaking to anyone else concerning the issues.

9. Interview the other parties. In the remaining investigation, follow the other parties' side of the story as well as the complainant's. Repeat the anti-retaliation policy and advice against speaking to anyone else.

10. Gather and review all relevant documents and evidence. Be sure to keep these in a file other than the employee's personnel file.

11. Ask the complainant and the other party in writing for any supplemental information. Provide a reasonable amount of time to respond.

12. Prepare an investigative report. List each allegation and describe the evidence supporting or contradicting the claims. Make findings of fact and recommend specific actions based on policy.

13. Management must make a preliminary determination. The employer must assess the results of the investigation and determine the appropriate response based on policy.

14. Inform the other party of any intended discipline. (More on this in Chapter 10.) Include the allegations, the evidence, and the findings. Clearly state the intended discipline. This individual should be given an opportunity to present any reasons why he or she should not be disciplined.

15. Advise the complainant that the employer has investigated the claim and state whether those claims were substantiated or not. If substantiated, inform the complainant that appropriate remedial measures have been taken and re-affirm the commitment to the anti-harassment and anti-retaliation policies. If unsubstantiated, state that the investigation is complete and the claims are unfounded. While this may not make you very popular, the reality is that a number of these cases become the classic "he said, she said."

The investigation should conclude with a written report indicating your findings and recommendations.

Other Things to Consider

Promote diversity in the workplace and treat everyone equally and with respect. Will this solve all of your employee issues? Of course not, but it will go a long way toward making your employees believe you are fair and encouraging them to share their issues with you.

I am often asked, "When should we call our lawyer?" There's no easy answer to this question; it depends on your tolerance for risk. Some good old-fashioned common sense helps here — clearly, if the employee begins to talk in legalese using terms like "hostile work environment" and/or you receive a letter or call from an attorney, a phone call to yours would be a good idea. Normally, however, if you manage your employees and respond to their issues, you will rarely hear from an attorney. I would definitely recommend the use of an in-house or outsourced human resources department. I would find someone you can use as a trusted advisor and let them help you determine the best time to contact counsel.

So what are the latest and greatest and things you should watch out for?

Retaliation

Have you ever played the game Whack-a-Mole? You know, the one where a mole sticks its head up and you hit it with a hammer? Plaintiff attorneys are a bit like this in that as soon as you "whack" them with a defense to one issue, they find another one and up they pop. Today, that issue is retaliation. Unfortunately, the courts don't really help us here by granting employees a greater ability to file cases based on retaliation. Now don't get me wrong, I know some companies deserve to be sued; the problem with retaliation is that it is easy for the employee to claim but difficult for you to prove you didn't do it. For example, let's say an employee complains about his supervisor. It is a formal complaint, and you investigate and discover that the supervisor is simply doing his job and holding the employee accountable. Eventually, you need to fire the employee. Guess what

— retaliation! Retaliation is difficult because it will often survive a summary judgment motion, which means you will have a jury trial unless you implement an arbitration policy (see Chapter 8).

Sexual Harassment

This used to be one of our Whack-a-Mole issues, but now with proper training and policies, you see much less of this type of case. Take complaints seriously, however, as they can proceed to court very quickly and be very expensive.

Wage and Hour

This, along with retaliation, is the latest Whack-a-Mole issue. While wage and hour laws have been with us since the 1930s, it is only recently that plaintiff attorneys have figured out that these can be great class-action cases. If you think this can't happen to you, think again. Do you pay at least minimum wage? Of course, you say. Do you calculate overtime correctly? You are sure you do. Well, maybe. What about breaks for hourly employees? Ever see an hourly employees eating lunch at their desks? If so, you may have a problem. Do your hourly employees clock out when they go to lunch and in when they return? No? Now you do have a problem. The point is that any one of these issues may be trivial from a cost standpoint, but enough of them put together — and considering that in some states you can go back as far as three years for willful violations — and the numbers add up quickly, getting an attorney's attention.

Facebook

Do you ever wonder what your employees do when they get home at night? I personally don't have time to care, but some people do, and where do they find out? Facebook and all the other social-media outlets. Is this legal? Can I decide not to hire someone because of what I see on Facebook? Can I fire someone for what I see? What if they call me a jerk on Twitter? Here is the answer: I don't know … yet. Here comes another round of Whack-a-Mole.

Religion

Religion is one of the protected areas of law that require you to accommodate the employee's needs. The other is employee disabilities. This means that unless it imposes an undue hardship on the organization, you need to accommodate an employee's religious needs. For the most part this is easy to do — but the real Whack-a-Mole issue is, what is a religion? What about a Wiccan? Stay tuned.

Disabilities

The American with Disabilities Act (ADA) also requires accommodations for disabilities as long as they don't cause an undue hardship for the organization. But what is a disability? Some, of course, are obvious, but not all. Outside assistance is recommended here.

The list of potential issues is endless and will continue to develop over time. My advice to you is, if you are unsure, call your HR consultant or an employment attorney.

Chapter 8
How to Stay Out of Court

There was a time we could resolve employment problems internally, and utilizing the court system was rarely an option. This began to change twenty or so years ago, and today just about any employee issue should be viewed as a potential lawsuit.

What would you do if one of your employees lied on his application for promotion and told you he had a degree when he didn't? Some of you might fire him, some might not. What if he did it again and again, and finally a fourth time? No kidding, this really happened. At some point he lost his job and sued. Did my customer "win" the case? Of course he did — at the cost of $100,000.

It is not always unavoidable and sometimes even preferable to allow a case to go to court. There have been times when a certain plaintiff's attorney has decided to send his kids to college by representing my client's ex-employees. The case I shared earlier was the first of three this attorney would file. The first case needed to go to court to show them that my customer would not roll over and settle. An employee's perception of a claim is his or her reality, and there is no shortage of plaintiff attorneys to take these cases. If there was a legal area in this country that I would consider legalized extortion, this would be it. Many of these cases are filed hoping and knowing that a company will quickly settle to avoid the cost.

A lawsuit from start to finish can easily cost more than $150,000, and that is if you "win." If you lose, you may be responsible for the plaintiff's attorney fees and, heaven forbid, a jury verdict. Consider also the time lost. Interrogatories, depositions, and trial can easily exceed a hundred hours per witness. Finally, consider the negative publicity. Depending upon your industry, this is publicity you don't need.

I am not an attorney and would never offer legal advice. There are a number of great employment attorneys who know a whole lot more than I do, so please call them with specific questions. What I do know, though, is that life at work is complicated, and if you don't believe me, consider these federal laws with which you need to comply. While this is by no means a complete list, I think it makes the point.

1. **Title VII of the Civil Rights Act of 1964** prohibits employment discrimination based on race, color, religion, sex, or national origin.
2. The **Age Discrimination in Employment Act (ADEA) of 1967** prohibits employment discrimination against those age forty and above.
3. The **Americans with Disabilities Act (ADA) of 1992** prohibits employment discrimination against persons with disabilities.
4. The **Immigration Reform and Control Act of 1986** covers the right to work in the United States and required documentation.
5. The **Fair Labor Standards Act** covers minimum wage and various wage and hour issues.
6. The **Equal Pay Act and the Ledbetter Act** cover equal pay for equal work between the sexes.
7. The **Employment Retirement Income and Security Act (ERISA)** covers various retirement and health-and-welfare plans.
8. **Workers' Compensation Laws** provide for the injured worker; requirements differ from state to state.
9. The **Wagner Act** covers various rules with respect to union activity.

10. The **Occupational Safety and Health Act** covers standards for workplace health and safety.
11. The **Drug Free Workplace Act** covers reporting requirements for employee drug use.
12. The **Family and Medical Leave Act** covers leaves of absence by employees.
13. The **Health Insurance Portability and Accountability Act** protects employees against dissemination of health data.
14. The **Pregnancy Discrimination Act** covers pregnancy and related conditions.
15. The **Uniformed Services Employment and Reemployment Rights Act** provides protections for returning service personnel.

Had enough? I believe the key to all of these laws is understanding the basic concept that you cannot treat one group of people different from others for reasons like:

- Age
- Physical or mental disability
- Medical condition
- Height/weight
- Marital status
- Sex
- Sexual orientation
- Pregnancy
- Religion
- Race/color
- National origin
- Veteran status
- Language

Please remember that this list is constantly evolving, and your state may have additional protected groups.

Unfortunately, you may be discriminating without even knowing you are doing it. There are two concepts in this area you should be familiar with. The first is called *disparate impact*, which is the result of policies that appear neutral on their face but have an adverse impact on a protected group. Many screening devices fall victim to disparate impact, which is why they need to be validated. The only defense to disparate impact is a business necessity, which can be difficult to prove.

The second is *disparate treatment*, which is treating similarly situated employees differently because of some prohibited factor. The only time this is permissible is when there is a bona fide occupational qualification (BFOQ) involved. A BFOQ allows for intentional discrimination if it is reasonably necessary to the employer's business. Again, this is hard to prove. An example might be hiring a male actor to play a male part. Ever seen *Tootsie*?

In any case, there has been and will be increased enforcement activity. A look at budget changes in some key government agencies makes this point.

Agency	2009 Budget (in millions)	2010 Budget (in millions)	% Change	2009 Staffing	2010 Staffing	% Change
National Labor Relations Board	$263	$283	8	1,680	1,685	.003
Equal Employment Opportunity Commission	$342	$367	7	2,256	2,556	13
Occupational Safety and Health Administration	$502	$564	12	2,165	2,360	9
Wage And Hour Division	$193	$228	18	1,283	1,571	22

These numbers clearly show that your odds of being audited by one or these agencies have increased. This chapter is about how to stay out of court, but of equal concern should be how to survive a government audit. The best strategy is to prevent one in the first place. In all cases, I recommend that you seek professional advice (attorney, human resources consultant, etc.) should you receive that audit notice. Normally, cooperation is the best approach, although I have lately seen a more belligerent attitude from many of these inspectors. All agencies are different, but the likely suspects you will encounter include:

- The Occupational Safety and Health Administration (OSHA) or your state equivalent
- Department of Wage and Hour Enforcement
- Department of Labor (various agencies)
- Equal Employment Opportunity Commission or your state's equivalent.

A government agency will contact you normally for one of three reasons: it's your lucky day (minimal chance), you didn't do something you were supposed to (moderate chance), or an employee, former employee, or customer complains and "blows the whistle" (excellent chance).

In any event, provide only what is asked for, but don't stonewall the investigation either. Don't let the audit scope expand. Make them stick to the original subject. Look like you know what you are doing even if you don't. Most importantly, stay calm!

Making sure your house is in order before a problem occurs is the best defense to a government audit. Here are some of the areas you should look at:

1. **Employee Handbooks**: Are you really doing what you say you are?
2. **Official Policies:** Do you have them for illegal harassment, ethics, whistle blowing, and complaint management?
3. **Legal Notices:** Do you have federal wage and hour, state wage and hour, and federal polygraph notices posted?

4. **Employee Records:** Are your records for attendance/ payroll, employment contracts, wage and hour, overtime, tips, authorization for deductions from pay, and I-9 up to date and accurate?
5. **Injury and Illness Prevention Program (IIPP):** If this program is required in your state, do you have one?
6. **Safety Records:** Is your OSHA log up to date with safety training, inspections, and corrective actions?
7. **Material Safety Data Sheets (MSDS):** Are they available for inspection?
8. **Emergency Action Plans:** Do they exist?
9. **COBRA:** Are you in compliance?
10. **Workers' Compensation:** Are your records up to date for reporting, accident investigation, and preemployment exams?
11. **Leave of Absence Policies:** Are yours in compliance with the Family Medical Leave Act (FMLA), Americans with Disabilities Act (ADA), and Employee Assistance Programs (EAP)?
12. **Sick Leave, Vacation, and Personal Time Off (PTO) Policies:** Do you pay unused balances upon termination?
13. **Wage and Hour Rules:** Are you in compliance with state and federal laws? Consider incentive compensation schemes, sales-incentive schemes, overtime, meal periods/ rest periods, minimum wage, callback pay, pay for travel time, prize and bonus pay, age discrimination, and child labor.

Had enough? But wait, there's more! Another area of concern is the proper classification of independent contractors vs. employees. Independent contractors should be able to give the answers indicated to the following questions in a way that would indicate their independent contractor status:

- Can you earn a profit or suffer a loss from the activity? *Yes*

- Are you told where to work by the hiring firm? *No*
- Can you offer your services to the general public? *Yes*
- Can you be fired by the hiring firm? *No*
- Does the hiring firm furnish the tools and materials you need to do the work? *No*
- Are you paid by the job or by the hour? *By the job*
- Can you work for more than one firm at a time? *Yes*
- Do you have a continuing relationship with the customer? *No*
- Does the hiring firm invest in your equipment and facilities? *No*
- Does the hiring firm pay your business and traveling expenses? *No*
- Do you have the right to quit without incurring liability? *No*
- Do you receive instructions from the hiring firm? *No*
- Are you told in what sequence or order to work by the hiring firm? *No*
- Do you receive training from the hiring firm? *No*
- Do you perform the services personally? *No*
- Can you hire and pay assistants? *Yes*
- Can you set your own working hours? *Yes*
- Do you work full-time for the hiring firm? *No*
- Are you required to provide regular oral or written progress reports to the hiring firm? *No*
- Are the services you provide an integral part of the hiring firm's day-to-day operations? *No*

Unfortunately, there is no number of right or wrong answers that will ensure you are in compliance, and the IRS will consider every case on its own merits. If you "guess" wrong, you could be liable for all past employment taxes — or perhaps even worse, employee benefits the contractor would be entitled to, such as stock options.

At a minimum, you need a handbook, and you must enforce the rules consistently to stay out of court. Most of the cases I handle revolve around the claim that one group is being treated differently than another. Consistency really is the key. Here's a quick look at what a handbook might include.

EMPLOYEE HANDBOOK
TABLE OF CONTENTS

Welcome
Our Core Values
Know Your Company
Our Customer-Relations Philosophy
Let's Communicate
> Our Employee-Relations Philosophy
> If You Have a Problem
> Purpose of This Employee Handbook

What You Can Expect from Us
> Equal Employment Opportunity
> Introductory Period
> Policy against Harassment
> Employee's Responsibility
> Employment At-Will Policy
> Solicitation and Distribution Rights
> Employee Classification
> Exempt Employees
> Work Schedule
> Timekeeping
> Overtime
> Open-Door Policy

Company Benefits
> Your Pay
> Paid Holidays
> Personal Time Off (PTO)
> Medical, Vision, Life, Accidental Death, Long-Term
>> Disability, Short-Term Disability, and Dental
>> Insurance
> COBRA
> State-Mandated Insurance Benefit Programs
> Social Security Insurance

Workers' Compensation Insurance
401(k) Plan
IRS Section 125 — Cafeteria Plan
Suggestion Program
Training and Education Assistance
Civic Duties
Jury Duty
Witness Duty
Domestic-Violence or Sexual-Assault Leave
    (California)
Voting
Unpaid Family School Partnership Leave (California)
Literacy Assistance (California)
Rehabilitation Leave
Pregnancy Disability Leave Of Absence (California)
Lactation Accommodation (California)
Family Medical Leave Act/California Family Rights Act
Personal Leave of Absence
Bereavement Leave
Military Leave of Absence
Company Paid Memberships and Publications
Professional Memberships and Affiliations
Publications
Bulletin Boards

What We Expect of You

Company Policies
Rules to Protect Us All
Absenteeism and Tardiness
Alcohol and Drug Policy
Standards of Conduct and Discipline
No Smoking Policy
Hiring of Relatives
Employee Dress and Personal Appearance
Computer Usage
Good Housekeeping
Off-Duty Employees
Second Jobs or Moonlighting

EMPLOYEE ACKNOWLEDGMENT AND AGREEMENT
Pre-Dispute Arbitration Policy & Acknowledgment

Every company will be different, and state laws vary, so always consult your HR consultant or attorney.

Another thought is to not rely on the concept of "at-will employment." Under this theory, employees can be terminated at will, and in some states this is actually found in the labor code. While this is a good idea and every handbook and offer letter should have language to this effect, there are so many exceptions to this concept that it will rarely keep you out of court. Given this, I would still recommend this type of language in your handbook:

> Please note that the Employee Handbook is not a contract of employment or an agreement, either express or implied. Although we hope that our employment relationship with you will be ongoing and rewarding for both of us, either the Company or you may terminate your employment at any time. Your employment is subject to our "Employment At-Will Policy" and may be terminated at any time, for any reason, with or without prior notice or cause, by either you or the Company.

Also, don't rely on probation periods as an opportunity to fire someone. Probationary periods are not really recognized by most court systems, and you cannot violate employees' legal rights regardless of their probationary status.

The best way to avoid court, in reality, is not to go there. One way to avoid this is by implementing an arbitration agreement. Arbitration agreements prevent employees from going to court and have a lot of benefits to both sides.

Here is an example:

PRE-DISPUTE ARBITRATION POLICY & ACKNOWLEDGMENT

The following is a lot of legalese that, unfortunately, is required by the legal system. We believe that our core values emphasize respect, which includes open, clear, and honest communication. Our entire dispute-resolution process is built on this assumption.

Please review this policy carefully. Your acknowledgment of the receipt of this policy indicates that you received a copy and that you understand it requires both the Company and you to arbitrate covered disputes set forth below rather than litigate. While this policy requires you to submit covered disputes to arbitration rather than to a court, you do not relinquish your right to utilize administrative agencies, such as the Equal Employment Opportunity Commission (EEOC) or equivalent state agencies. This also does not affect your right to utilize the workers' compensation system in your state. Please read the following statements carefully.

The Company and the Employee shall submit to binding arbitration all disputes and claims that they have against each other that would otherwise be subject to jurisdiction by a state or federal court of law, or by any federal or state agency having adjudicative jurisdiction over such claims. These include but are not limited to the following:

1.   All disputes and claims that arise out of or relate in any manner to

the Employee's application for
employment or employment with
the Company;

2.   Any dispute over the termination
of the Employee's employment
with the Company; and/or

3.   All disputes concerning any
agreement or alleged agreement
between the Employee and the
Company, or any legal dispute of
any type.

This Pre-Dispute Arbitration Policy ("Policy") includes
all disputes and claims that either the Company or the
Employee have against the other, including but not limited
to: contract claims; tort claims; trade-secret claims; wage
claims; breach-of-confidentiality claims; claims involving
laws against discrimination, including discrimination based
on race, sex, sexual orientation, religion, national origin,
age, marital status, handicap, disability, medical condition,
gender, or harassment on any of the foregoing grounds
(whether allegedly in violation of federal or state law); claims
involving co-employees; and/or claims for benefits, except
as excluded herein; and claims for an alleged violation of
any federal, state, or other governmental law, common law,
statute, regulation or ordinance, including but not limited to:
Title VII of the Civil Rights Act of 1964, the California Fair
Employment and Housing Act, the Fair Labor Standards Act,
the Equal Pay Act, the Americans with Disabilities Act, the
Age Discrimination in Employment Act, the California Family
Rights Act, the Family Medical Leave Act, the California
Labor Code Private Attorneys General Act of 2004, and the
Labor Management Relations Act, including claims under
all similar state laws in all states in which the Company
has employees. Each party hereto waives any right to have
any such dispute or claim heard in any forum other than
the arbitration forum set forth in this Policy, except for the
right of the Employee to file with the EEOC, the California

Department of Fair Employment and Housing (DFEH), or any similar state agency in any state in which the employee works for the Company; however, after review by the EEOC or state agency is completed, the Employee must exhaust the arbitration procedure contained in this Policy. **Both parties expressly waive their respective right to trial by jury.**

In addition, requests for temporary restraining orders and/or preliminary injunctions by either the Employee or the Company, where such temporary equitable relief would otherwise be authorized by law, shall be submitted to arbitration for emergency treatment. The arbitration administrator shall select a neutral hearing officer to hear the emergency request. The hearing officer shall apply the applicable law and legal standards as if this matter were heard in a court of law in the state in which the Employee works for the Company.

The arbitrator shall have exclusive authority to resolve any dispute relating to the formation, interpretation, applicability, or enforceability of this Policy, including but not limited to any claim that all or any part of this Policy is void or voidable.

Excluded Claims: Claims with respect to the Employee Retirement Income Security Act (ERISA), workers' compensation benefits, worker disability compensation, claims under the National Labor Relations Act that are brought before the National Labor Relations Board, or unemployment compensation benefits are not covered by this Policy. Claims that the Company retaliated against an employee for filing state unemployment insurance, workers' compensation, or disability compensation are subject to arbitration hereunder. Either party may also bring an action in any court of competent jurisdiction to compel arbitration of a matter covered by this Policy and to enforce an arbitration award.

Notice of Claim: The aggrieved party must file a written demand for arbitration with the American Arbitration Association and serve a copy on the other party within thirty (30) days after the conclusion of the Level 4 proceedings, except that in any matter involving a statutory or common-law claim the demand for arbitration must be filed and served no later than the expiration of the statute of limitations applicable to the claim at issue. In the case of any notice of claim to be served on the Company, such notice shall be delivered to xxx c/o Vice President of Human Resources and Administration, 2465 Campus Drive, Irvine CA 92612. In the case of any notice of claim to be served on the employee, such notice shall be delivered to the employee's last known address on file with the Company. All notices of claim shall be served by certified mail, return receipt requested, or by a recognized overnight delivery service.

AAA Rules: The arbitration shall be conducted consistent with the rules of the American Arbitration Association (AAA) as set forth in the Employment Arbitration Rules and Mediation Procedures, effective as of November 1, 2009, and as they may be amended from time to time.[1] A copy of the AAA Rules is attached. In the event that the AAA Rules are inconsistent with any provision of this Policy or the Federal Arbitration Act ("FAA"), the provisions of this Policy and the FAA shall govern. In the event that the FAA does not apply, then the version of the Uniform Arbitration Act adopted in the State where the employee worked for the Company shall apply.

Applicable Law: The substantive laws of the state in which the Employee works for the Company shall be used by the arbitrator to determine the respective rights and obligations of the parties hereto with respect to any state cause of action, and with respect to any federal cause

---

1   Any amendments to the AAA Rules are available in the Human Resources office and on the AAA website: *http://www.adr.org*.

of action, the federal substantive law will be applicable; provided, however, only to the extent they do not conflict with the Federal Arbitration Act, and in such event, FAA law shall prevail. The arbitrator is entitled to grant any remedy that a court or jury hearing the case could grant under the applicable state or federal law. The Company shall pay the reasonable fees of the arbitrator and the expenses associated with the arbitration, to the extent that such fees and expenses exceed the amount the Employee would have incurred had the claim(s) been brought in the state or federal court having jurisdiction over the claim(s). Subject to the power of the arbitrator to award costs, the Employee shall pay to the arbitrator or the arbitration service the fees that he would have paid in state or federal court to pursue the case. Each party will pay his/her/its own attorney's fees and expenses associated with the arbitration, subject to the right of the arbitrator to award such fees and costs in accordance with the substantive law applicable to the claim(s) at issue.

With respect to all claims not arising from or based upon a state or federal statute (or public policy based on state or federal law), and with respect to non-employment related claims, the parties shall each pay his/her/its pro-rata share of the fees of the AAA and, as established by the arbitrator, of the arbitrator's expenses and fees.

Selection of Arbitrator: A neutral arbitrator with at least ten (10) years of experience in deciding disputes of the type being submitted under the law of the state in which the Employee works for the Company shall be mutually selected by the parties. In the event the parties are unable to mutually agree upon an arbitrator, the parties shall select an arbitrator as provided for by the AAA rules.

Hearing Location, Discovery Rights, and Other Procedures: Except as the parties may otherwise agree, the hearing will be held in the state in which the employee was employed by the Company at the time the claim arose. Each party will be able to serve discovery on the other party consisting of a request for production of documents and up to twenty-five (25) interrogatories and to take one deposition. The arbitrator shall have the authority to permit additional discovery as may be warranted by the dispute at issue consistent with the expedited and simplified nature of arbitration proceedings. At least thirty (30) days before the arbitration hearing, the parties will exchange lists of proposed witnesses, including any experts, and copies of any exhibits intended to be used at the arbitration. Either party may request such remedies and damages that are allowed by applicable federal law or the law of the state in which Employee works for the Company. The parties shall be entitled to submit briefs to the arbitrator within thirty (30) days of the close of the hearing. A written arbitration decision with a statement of the reasons for the award shall be issued by the arbitrator. To the extent applicable in civil actions in the federal courts in the state in which the arbitration is held, all rules of pleading, rules of evidence, and rights to resolution of the disputes by motions to dismiss or motions for summary judgment shall be applicable. Resolution of the dispute shall be based solely on the controlling law, and the arbitrator shall not invoke any basis (including but not limited to notions of "just cause") other than such controlling law. The arbitrator shall decide the case based on the evidence presented, even if one party fails to appear.

Reconsideration Rights: The selected arbitrator must agree to retain jurisdiction after issuing a written arbitration decision for at least twenty (20) days in order to allow either party to file a request for reconsideration. If no such request is made, the decision and award will be final and binding and no further review will be provided under this Policy. In the event either party shall file with the arbitrator a request to reconsider the arbitrator's decision within said twenty (20) day period, the arbitrator will retain jurisdiction until such time as a decision on said request for reconsideration is issued. After a request for reconsideration is filed, the opposing party shall have twenty (20) days to submit a brief. The arbitrator shall consider the request and any briefs and either confirm or change the previously issued arbitration decision. The final decision of the initial arbitrator, issued after a request for reconsideration, may be subject to an additional review at the written request of either party served on the other within twenty (20) days after issuance of the decision on reconsideration. That review shall be submitted to a retired Justice of the Supreme Court or the intermediate Court of Appeal or the federal court sitting in the state in which Employee worked for the Company, who shall review the first arbitrator's decision and apply the same standard of review which would be applied by a federal appellate court reviewing a decision of a trial court sitting without a jury. The second arbitrator shall be mutually selected from a panel of retired judges, having at least five (5) years service, obtained from the AAA. Subject to the right of the second arbitrator to allocate fees and expenses for a frivolous appeal, the fees and expenses for such appeal shall be borne by the Company, except for any appellate fees that the Employee would normally pay for an appeal under state court appeal rules and the Employee will pay those fees to the arbitrator or the arbitration service.

With respect to all claims not arising from or based upon a state or federal statute (or public policy based on state or federal law), and with respect to non-employment related claims, the parties shall each pay his/her/its pro-rata share, as established by the second arbitrator, of the second arbitrator's expenses and fees.

Complete Policy: This Policy constitutes the complete policy as of the date set forth below with regard to dispute resolution, and there are no other agreements as to dispute resolution, either oral or written. It shall be interpreted and construed pursuant to the provisions of the AAA. If any provision of this Policy is found to be void or otherwise unenforceable, in whole or in part, it shall not affect the validity of the remainder of the Policy, which will remain in full force and effect.

Voluntary Agreement: The Employee acknowledges that he/she has knowingly and voluntarily agreed to this Policy without reliance on any provisions or representations by the Company other than those contained herein. The Employee further acknowledges that he/she has been given the opportunity to discuss this Policy with Human Resources and/or his/her legal counsel prior to signing this Policy.

Effective Date of Policy: This Policy shall become effective as to any claim or dispute that arises on or after January 1, 2011. This Policy shall continue in effect indefinitely, except that the Company may modify or terminate this Policy as to future disputes or claims, upon a minimum of forty-five (45) days written notice prior to the effective date of the modification or termination. In addition, any modification or termination shall only be effective with respect to any claim or dispute arising after the effective date of the modification or termination.

I acknowledge receipt of the forgoing Arbitration Policy and AAA Rules, and understand that it provides for binding arbitration of all disputes as defined in the Policy. I also understand that as a result of this Arbitration Policy, I am not entitled to a trial by jury of any claim I or the Company may have against each other.

I further understand that nothing in the Policy alters the at-will status of my employment.

Date: ____   _____

                                    Employee Signature

The advantages of arbitration are many. While a court case may take two to three years to resolve, arbitration can be done in months. While a court case can easily exceed $150,000, my experience is that arbitration costs around $30,000. Still not cheap, but certainly better. There's no risk of a runaway jury, since there is no jury. Finally, punitive damages, while available in arbitration, are unlikely unless you have really done something egregious to the employee. I started one just yesterday that ended with the employee agreeing to settle for a neutral offer letter. Does this happen often? No, but you never know.

Sometimes, no matter what you do, you will still end up in court. Here are some examples:

- An employee goes on a medical leave and never returns — doesn't call, just disappears. Did my customer get sued? Yes.
- An employee quits because he doesn't like his boss. Can he sue? Yes, and he did.
- An employee punches the time card of another employee. She is terminated. Did she sue? You bet!
- An employee takes a company vehicle home, runs personal errands, gets into an accident, and is terminated. Sue? Yup.
- How about the boss who heard that one of his employees got breast implants, ran up the stairs to her work area, and yelled, "Where is she? I need to see them!" Did we get sued? Well, actually ... no! You just never know.

Chapter 9
How to Train Them

//

Let's be honest. Have you ever been sufficiently trained? I have always subscribed to the concept of being a lifelong learner, and I appreciate any training I can get. While each employee's situation will be different, we need to ask how much training is really required and whether the results justify the expense.

In looking at employee training, I would suggest you ask the following questions: Why are we doing this training? Is it to provide knew skills, or is it in response to an employee performance problem? Is training really the solution to the employee's performance problem? Oftentimes, when an employee is not performing, the natural assumption is that the problem is lack of training. I would suggest that before you reach this conclusion, you consider whether the employee is willing and/or able to do the job. Willingness is the interest, motivation, and confidence to improve, whereas ability is the knowledge, skill, and resources to improve.

Consider the following chart.

Low Ability & High Willingness

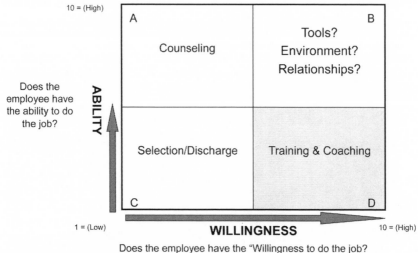

Figure 9.1

This willingness and ability table is a useful tool when trying to decide if a performance issue represents an employee's lack of willingness to perform or is really because of lack of ability. We will go over this more in the next chapter, but assuming the employee's willingness is high but ability is low, it is definitely time to train. Once we have reached this conclusion, we need to follow a training sequence as is illustrated below.

Figure 9.2

Are the goals of the training clear and realistic? Far too often we enter into training without considering its real goal. Are you trying to provide information? Improve skills? Do you expect a real change in performance?

We have briefly discussed the need for training, but how do we know if the employee is ready? The necessary employee characteristics to ensure readiness of training include:

- Ability to learn the subject matter
- Favorable attitudes toward the training
- Motivation to learn

All of these need to be present for training to be a success. The planned training program should directly relate to the needs identified by the needs assessment, which we have already discussed. Effective training objectives have three components: what the employee is expected to do, the quality or level of performance that is acceptable, and the conditions under which the trainee is expected to apply what is learned.

Once we are convinced that your employee can and is willing to learn, it is time to figure out what the best training method would be. A wide variety of methods are available for conducting training, such as:

- Classroom training
- Training videos
- Role-plays
- Case studies
- Computer-based training
- Learning games
- Experiential programs

Developing training internally is expensive and, for most organizations, not a cost-effective approach. There are a variety of outside sources available, and I would recommend that you contact the American Society of Training and Development (http://www. astd.org) with your specific training needs.

Did the training work? This is the tricky part of the training sequence and the most difficult to measure. Some measures of training success might include:

- **Trainee satisfaction with the program**. This is the lowest level of training success and is often more a function of the trainer's popularity than actual training effectiveness.
- **Knowledge or abilities learned**. Learning is an improvement and a step above employee satisfaction. It is very possible the trainees were not satisfied yet learned what you hoped they would.
- **Use of new skills and behaviors on the job**. Here is the first real step to success. Did they take the skills they learned and try to use them, recognizing that it would feel strange and unnatural?

- **Improvements in individual performance**. Success! This is what we were trying to achieve.
- **Improvements in organizational performance**. Here we really justify our investment.

At the end of the day, training needs to improve performance; that is the bottom-line measurement. For more information on the best of the outsourced training providers, check out this website: http://www.trainingindustry.com/top-20-main-listing-page.aspx.

Chapter 10
How to Discipline and Fire Them

//

In many ways, this was the most challenging chapter to write for this book. After thirty years in human resources, I have more stories to tell than I can possible cram into this little volume. For example, I mentioned in the opening about my customer whose employee staged a hunger strike. Ultimately, he had to be fired for reasons that had nothing to do with his hunger strike. Guess what? He claimed retaliation. Four years later, we settled this gentleman's case for very little money and all kinds of aggravation.

Then there was the employee running a business out of her office. Unfortunately it wasn't *our* business. She was indignant when she was fired. She didn't understand the concept of "stealing time." Then, of course, there are the employees who threaten their supervisors and co-workers. Or the ones who refuse to follow simple policies and procedures. And let's not forget the ones who are intoxicated or on drugs at work. All in all, these are the easy ones.

In some ways this is the most difficult chapter to write because of the angst that goes into every disciplinary situation. It is not easy, not pleasant, and often doesn't end well for you and certainly not for the employee. So for the purposes of this chapter, let's look at two different activities that require discipline: performance-related issues vs. dysfunctional behavior. I separate these two because your approach to them will be very different.

For example we have all seen great people who were really nice and hardworking, they just couldn't do their jobs. No doubt you have also seen the liar, thief, drinker, cheater, and otherwise nasty human being who you couldn't wait to see leave. Let's start with the tough one: the good folks who simply can't do the job.

Let's once again review our chart about ability and willingness:

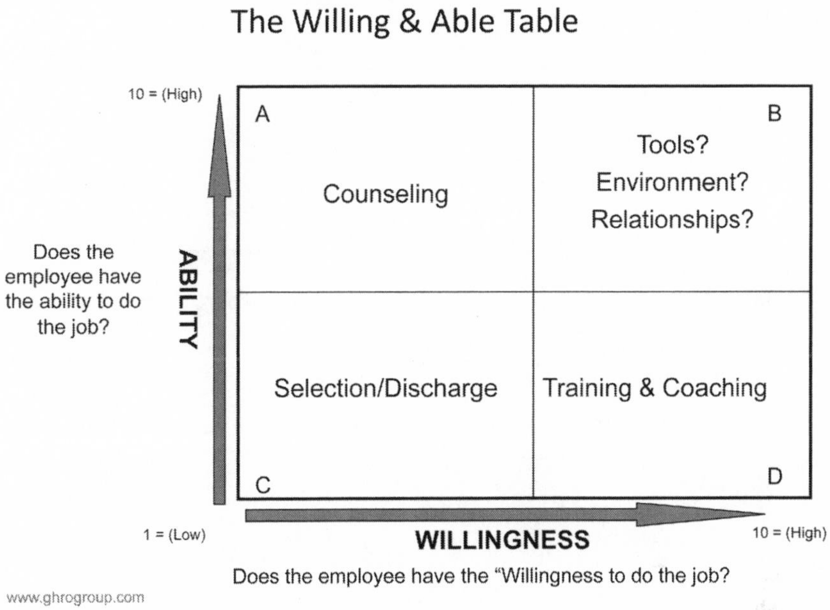

The Willing & Able Table

Figure 10.1

If someone has the ability to do the job and isn't performing, we coach and train that individual (quadrant D). If that doesn't work and we know he or she has been trained, we provide counseling (quadrant A). More on this in a minute. If the individual has neither the ability nor the willingness, we move on to discharge (quadrant C).

So the first question you have to ask yourself is, when is it appropriate to coach and/or counsel?

Performance

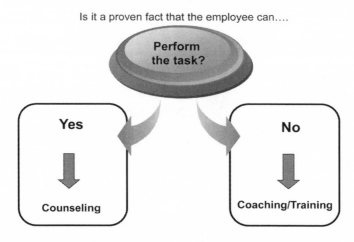

Is it a proven fact that the employee can....

Perform the task?

Yes → Counseling

No → Coaching/Training

Figure 10.2

This is a critical question to ask because the wrong decision could have a devastating impact on the employee. If you are not *absolutely* sure he or she can perform the task, I would consider more training. Assuming the answer to this question is yes, then we should coach first, and then finally counsel.

Low Ability & High Willingness

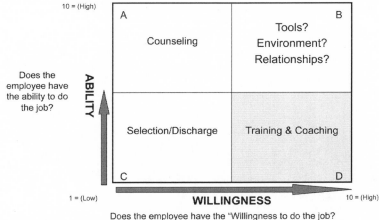

Figure 10.3

You Need To Be a Coach

So what is coaching? Like a sports coach, you point out the things the employee is doing well and the things that he or she is not doing so well. Here are some characteristics of a good coach:

Characteristics of a Good Coach

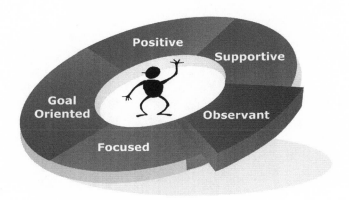

www.ghrogroup.com

Figure 10.4

Coaching is the process of observing employee performance, looking for both the good and bad, and bringing these things to the employee's attention.

Coaching

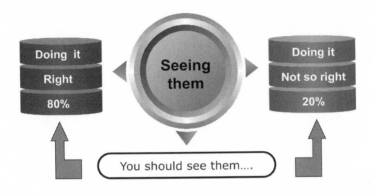

Figure 10.5

We recommend you catch them doing it right 80 percent of the time and only spend 20 percent on the "not so right." Coaching just takes a minute. For example, you see an employee doing something that will prove very helpful to the customer.

Atta Way Coaching

80% Doing it Right!

4. No Strings Attached

3. Keep it Performance Focused

2. Give Encouragement

1. State the Specific

www.ghrogroup.com

Figure 10.6

1. **State the specific thing the employee is doing that you are appreciative of.** Speaking in generalities is a mistake, since most people won't really understand why they are getting the praise. For example, "Nichole, thanks so much for catching that mistake in our customer's report. You saved me a lot of embarrassment, and I really appreciate it."
2. **Give encouragement.** Make sure the employee understands how much this means to you and the customer. When employees understand why this is important, it puts the "Atta way" in context.
3. **Keep it performance-focused.** Discuss the activity the person performed, not the person.
4. **No strings attached.** Never include a but. For example, "John, I really appreciate you providing that report to our

customer early, since it helped them solve a problem ... but there was a typo when there shouldn't be." The big but sends a mixed message, which can be confusing.

When you see the employee doing something wrong:

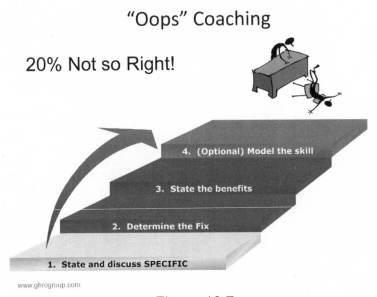

"Oops" Coaching

20% Not so Right!

4. (Optional) Model the skill

3. State the benefits

2. Determine the Fix

1. State and discuss SPECIFIC

www.ghrogroup.com

Figure 10.7

1. **State and discuss specifics**. Again, nothing is more powerful than specific examples.
2. **Determine the fix**. This is a quick discussion, and you can tell the employee what is expected and how to fix the problem.
3. **State the benefits**. Most people will comply with our requests and company policies if they understand the reasons why.
4. **Model the skill**, if it is appropriate, or show the employee the proper way to perform the task.

You Need To Be a Counselor

Sometimes, unfortunately, coaching does not work. Then we have to move to counseling. Counseling is used when coaching fails and is a form of communication that gives the employee the information needed to change unproductive behavior. It involves changing negative behaviors and is a *joint* problem-solving discussion. Counseling should end with *agreed* action between you and the employee. It should not be a one-way discussion.

Counseling employees is like any other process and consists of the following steps:

1. **Let the employee know that in general, he or she is doing a good job**. However, there is one thing (or more) that must change for the individual to stay employed.
2. **State the problem *specifically***. Ask the employee for input. Find out what they think of the problem, or if they think it is a problem at all.
3. **Playback the employee's concerns and summarize to make sure you really understand the issue**. This is also known as active listening.
4. **Use a "regardless" ramification statement**. So for example, "I understand that you feel like you haven't received the amount of training you think you need, and we have discussed this before. Regardless of this, you need to improve this phase of your performance or we will be forced to terminate your employment."
5. **Seek the employee's solution**. This will create ownership on the employee's part, giving the solution greater chance of success.
6. **Select the best option**. Set up a follow-up time/plan that the employee must verbally agree to.
7. **Restate #1**.
8. **Record the meeting and place in employee's file**.

That's it! So how many times should you use this approach? It depends on the performance issue, the number of times you have discussed it in the past, and your company's culture and philosophy. In any case, the discussions need to be documented and consistent with your policy.

Everything we have discussed thus far may lead at some point to *progressive discipline*, an escalating process of dealing with failure to perform to expectations or to change behavior. It typically consists of several steps. I would recommend the following sequence:

1. **Coaching Conversation.** As previously discussed, a coaching conversation is a quick "oops" counseling, and most of the time this is sufficient to change behavior.
2. **Counseling Session.** This is often called a *documented verbal warning.* Since coaching failed, counseling is required, and as such you are starting the formal discipline process.
3. **Written Warning.** A written warning is very much like the counseling session, however, because it is the next step of the process the employee needs to realize that the severity of the discipline has increased.
4. **Day of Reflection.** The supervisor will provide the employee with a day off with pay to decide if this is the right environment for him or her. The employee will return with a either a letter of resignation or a letter of commitment agreeing to modify behavior to acceptable standards by following a written plan that he or she will develop.
5. **Termination**. If the day of reflection fails, this is the end of the road.

The format for a modification agreement could look like this:

<u>EMPLOYEE BEHAVIOR MODIFICATION AGREEMENT</u>

Employee Name _____ Date _____

Supervisor Name _____ Department _____

☐ Documented Verbal Counseling   ☐ Written Warning   ☐ Day of Reflection   ☐ Termination

The purpose of this Employee Behavior Modification Agreement is to document performance issues and our agreed-upon solution to correct these issues.

The performance issue(s) are listed below: (Supervisor, write your objectives.)

_____

_____

_____

The agreed-upon solutions to these performance issue(s) are listed below. (Supervisor, write agreed-upon performance standards). These should be specific, measurable, achievable, and results driven, with time frame in which to complete them.

_____

Just a reminder, I last ☐ coached ☐ counseled you on these issues on: (date) _____

I have confidence that if you follow through on your commitment to the above agreed-upon performance standards, your performance will improve to meet company expectations. However, if you do not follow through on your stated commitments, you will receive further disciplinary action, up to and including termination. The next step would be:

☐ Documented Verbal   ☐ Written Warning   ☐ Day of Reflection   ☐ Termination
Counseling

Next review (if any) is scheduled on: _____

I have received a copy of this document.

_____
Employee Signature   Date

_____
Supervisor/Manager Signature   Date

_____
Human Resources Signature   Date

My thanks to Nichole DeGidio and Ronnie Glassman with GHRO for their help on this subject.

This should be documented and put into the employee's file.

The goal of this process is to change employee behavior and not to fire anyone, especially after taking the time to coach and counsel them. Unfortunately, terminations do occur. Some employees will just not be able to perform regardless of all the coaching in the world. At some point in time, we must respectfully separate the employee and move on.

Terminating the Employee

Firing an employee is never easy, and you should remember the following steps:

1. **Don't debate or negotiate**. Once the decision to terminate the employee is made, don't debate or negotiate with the employee. This really is not the time. The conversation with the employee should not take more than five to ten minutes. Any more and things can become more uncomfortable than they already are.
2. **Never lose your temper**. It is not uncommon for the employee to lose his or hers, but you should always take the high road. Allowing the employee to vent a little is okay, but remember the five-to-ten-minutes rule.
3. **Tackle disciplinary action head on; do not avoid it**. Avoiding it never works. At best, the behavior will stay the same, and more likely it will get worse. Also, other employees know what is going on and are looking to you for leadership. Failure to provide it could cause others to lose respect for you.
4. **Never play therapist, unless of course you are a therapist**. Even then, it isn't time to figure out the why of things. Just execute this and get it over with.
5. **Shut down computer systems, key cards, and cell phones**. I would suggest this be done while you are in the meeting with the employee or as soon thereafter as possible. For crying out loud, though, don't do it ahead of time. What kind of signal does that send to everyone else?

6. **Have all of the required paperwork ready**. States have different requirements regarding final pay, final termination letter, etc. Take the time to find out about these in advance. Also, decide how you will handle reference checks and inform the employee of this during the meeting. Here is an excellent website concerning final paychecks: http://www.nolo.com/legal-encyclopedia/article-29882.html.

7. **Treat the employee respectfully**. While it may be necessary at times to have security escort an employee out of the building and send his or her personal belongings later, this is seldom the preferred approach. I would rather you give the individual time to pack up, say good-bye to coworkers, etc. Rarely, though, should this exceed more than a few hours.

8. **Err on the side of caution**. If you think the employee may be dangerous, alert local law-enforcement or private security before termination. Better safe than sorry. Here are some of the warning signs to look out for:

   a. **History of Violence**: Fascination with weapons, acts of violence, or both; demonstrated violence toward inanimate objects; evidence of earlier violent behavior

   b. **Threatening Behavior**: States intention to hurt someone (can be verbal or written); holds grudges.

   c. **Excessive Behavior**: Phone calls; gift giving; escalating threats that appear well planned; preoccupation with violence.

   d. **Intimidating Behavior**: Argumentative; displays unwarranted anger; uncooperative; impulsive; easily frustrated; challenges peers and authority figures.

   e. **Increase in Personal Stress**: An unreciprocated romantic obsession; serious family or financial problems.

   f. **Negative Personality Characteristics**: Suspicious of others; believes he or she is entitled to something; cannot take criticism; feels victimized; shows a lack of concern for the safety or well-being of others; blames others for his problems or mistakes; low self-esteem; marked changes in mood or behavior; extreme or bizarre behavior; irrational beliefs and ideas; appears depressed or expresses hopelessness or heightened anxiety; marked decline in work performance; socially isolated; history of negative interpersonal relationships; few family or friends; sees the company as a "family"; has an obsessive involvement with his or her job; abuses drugs or alcohol.

9. **Remember the survivors**. You will need to deal with those who remain. They will need time to grieve the loss of their teammate. Even if you did not think this individual was popular, you may be surprised by the remaining employees' reactions. Obviously you cannot share too many details of the departure — "John left for other opportunities" is a time-tested standard line and should be sufficient to protect the departing employee's dignity and privacy. Allow people time to work through their feelings, and be sensitive to their mood changes.

This is a long list, to be sure, and terminating an employee is never easy. Unfortunately it will have to be done from time to time.

Performance-related terminations are, in my opinion, the most difficult because usually the employee is really trying to meet your expectations. The second category I mentioned earlier was that of dysfunctional behavior. In these cases, termination is immediate after confirmation of the event through your investigation. While many things can constitute dysfunctional behavior, here is a partial list.

Dishonesty

While dishonesty is somewhat vague, I would recommend you define it in your employee handbook or company policies. Your culture will dictate the extent to which dishonesty will be a terminable offense. I once had an employee drive off our work site with a truck full of copper wire he had stolen from the building he worked in.

When terminated, he told me he was going to get himself a lawyer. I smiled and said, "Well, I have lots of them."

Falsification of Records

Falsifying any work, personnel, or other business records, specifically including time cards, either yours or another employee's, can all be terminable offenses. Punching in and out for your friend is a common problem in organizations that use time clocks. Switching to biometric clocks can eliminate this problem. Again, your culture and type of business will dictate your tolerance level for falsification.

Controlled Substances

Possession, consumption, or being under the influence of alcohol or a controlled substance during working hours, on company premises, in company vehicles or equipment, or at any time while an employee is on company business would be considered dysfunctional behavior and grounds for termination.

Fighting or Threatening Another Employee

I have found the threatening part to be interesting. One person's view of a threat can be very different from another's, so I would suggest running this by a third party before taking action. I once had an employee chase another around the factory with a belt because of a Super Bowl bet.

Gambling

Gambling at work or on work premises can be grounds for termination. Of course if you run a casino this may or may not be an issue.

Insubordination or Disobedience

Failure to comply with a reasonable management directive can be considered dysfunctional behavior. The key word here is *reasonable*. Never terminate an employee who believes his or her safety is put in jeopardy by following a manager's directive. Investigate and then decide.

Inappropriate Language at Work

Swearing or verbal abuse while at work can be a terminable offense. If you remember my Whack-a-Mole discussion previously, workplace bullying is going to become the next issue for plaintiff's attorneys. Civil and respectful behavior should be the standard in the workplace.

Discrimination

Illegal discrimination against or illegal harassment of co-workers, management, customers or members of the public encountered during work can be considered dysfunctional behavior and grounds for termination.

Weapons

Possession of a firearm, weapon, or other hazardous or dangerous device or substance while working for the company or on company premises or equipment can be grounds for termination.

Violation of Safety Rules and Policies

You can always discipline an employee for failure to follow safety rules. You cannot discipline them however for having an accident or filing for workers' compensation.

Criminal Behavior

Pleading nolo contendere or guilty to, or being convicted of, any crime other than a minor traffic violation can be considered grounds for termination. Again, this one will be industry specific and may or may not apply.

Sleeping on the Job

My only caution here is to be sure there is no physical disability that causes the employee to fall asleep. If there is, a reasonable accommodation may be required.

Absenteeism

Excessive unscheduled absenteeism, unscheduled tardiness, or failure to report in when absent or late for work can be a terminable offense. You have the right to establish reasonable rules regarding attendance so long as you enforce those rules consistently. This is the main weakness I see in most company's attendance policies, and it will come back to bite you every time. Also make sure there are no disability issues that are causing the employee to miss work. If so, there may be a need to accommodate.

Breach of Confidentiality

Unauthorized disclosure of or use of information regarding company business or other confidential company information can be grounds for termination. If you don't have a confidentiality agreement in your workplace, I would suggest you implement one.

Performing Work of a Personal Nature during Working Time

Yes, it is wrong to run another business using the company computer. I once had an employee run a brothel in his RV on company premises. He couldn't figure out the problem since he said he was limiting the activity to breaks and lunch.

Policy Violation

As long as you've specified them ahead of time, violation of particular company policies may be terminable. This is a bit of a grey area. What you consider terminable, a judge or jury may not. Things also change over time. As I sit on a plane working on this book, I can remember a time when flight attendants were called stewardesses and were always young, attractive women. Most airlines had policies requiring a certain age, height, weight etc. Times have changed and I would check with your HR consultant or attorney prior to publishing your policies.

The bottom line is that even today, in our litigious environment, the secret is to treat people fairly and consistently. While that may not be easy to do, it will eliminate a lot of problems in the long run.

Finally, let me add a few thoughts about layoffs and reductions in force. While fundamentally you would execute these in the same way as any other termination, the real question is who are the correct people to let go. There are a number of ways to determine whom to reduce:

- Seniority
- Performance
- Function
- Department

All of these are fine so long as you are not letting someone go for one of the protected reasons we have discussed previously. Again, document, document, and then document again to ensure that you can prove your nondiscriminatory intent should you need to.

Chapter 11
How to Deal With the Unions

///

Unions today make up a very small part of the workforce. In the 1950s, union membership stood at around 35 percent of the working population. Today the number is less than 12 percent, with most of these in the public sector. Why the fall? I would like to say it is because you have all read my book and are using excellent HR practices that keep people from wanting to join unions. Wishful thinking. In fact, there are a number of reasons, including these:

- Many of the issues that originally brought unions to the workplace, such as minimum wages, child labor, and safety, have all been legislated both federally and locally.
- A number of industries where unions once dominated, such as textile and steel, have moved offshore.
- The old concept of "personnel" evolved into the practice of human resources , and companies made a much greater effort to meet the needs of their employees, thus giving them much less reason to organize.

Given the above, I would suggest that in the twenty-first century, if you wake up one morning to find a union at your door, it will constitute a failure of management not of the employees. Unfortunately, if you do wake up that morning with this new problem, your work is really cut out for you.

Labor Relations Management

Like most things in human resources, labor-relations management is a process consisting of three steps:

1. Union organizing
2. Collective bargaining
3. Contract administration

Union Organizing

The union organizing process is the attempt by the union to convince a sufficient number (30 percent) of employees to sign authorization cards allowing for an election. While you may or may not know this is going on (often you will not), the union will meet with individuals and groups, often offsite, to try to convince them of the advantages of joining the union. Once the union supporters have sufficient signatures, they will petition the National Labor Relations Board to hold an election. At that point, let the games begin.

The election campaign will be a lively one, and there are a number of things you should remember regarding your conduct — the dos and don'ts, if you will.

What you can do:

- You can talk to your employees.
- You can give your opinion.
- You can run your operation in the same way you have done in the past.
- You can share your personal experience with unions.
- You can tell your employees that in your opinion, the union is not good for them and why.
- You can tell them that even if the union is voted in, it doesn't mean they will get anything more. The company pays the wages and benefits for the employees, not the union.

- You can tell them that just because they may have signed a card, they are not obligated to support the union. There will be an election, which is by secret ballot.
- You can tell them that if they have been told they will have to join the union, that is false. This is a negotiated item.
- You can tell them that they may have to quit working even if they don't want to. They may have to strike and lose wages. They may have to march in a picket line. It could be cold.
- You can tell them if they strike, they may be replaced. Their chances of "getting ahead" are smaller in a union since everyone is treated the same.
- You can post news stories about union activities on the bulletin board.
- You can discuss the union's strike history.
- You can mention the amount of union dues.
- You can tell employees that they don't have to talk to the union representatives if they don't want to.

There are also a number of things you cannot do:

- You cannot question employees about the union.
- You cannot discriminate against them because they want to or are thinking of joining the union.
- You cannot spy on their meetings.
- You cannot threaten them in any way.
- You cannot promise them benefits or grant additional benefits if they don't join.
- You cannot visit them at their homes to discuss union issues.

That's it. As you can see, the list of what you can do is much longer than what you cannot. Take advantage of this and talk to your folks.

Collective Bargaining

Let's assume for the moment that you have lost the election. Now what? You are now entering the phase where you must negotiate in good faith toward the goal of reaching a collective-bargaining agreement or union contract. Generally, you must negotiate things like:

- Rates of pay
- Overtime
- Retirement benefits
- Health and welfare benefits
- Holidays
- Vacation
- Shifts
- Layoffs
- Seniority
- Safety
- Work rules
- Grievance procedures

While this is not an all-inclusive list, it is indicative of the issues you will be discussing with the union. While there are many different styles of negotiating, as a rule I would consider the following;

- **Develop a solid working relationship early on in the process with the Union Rep.** Yelling and screaming may feel good, but it generally does not help the process move along.
- **Try to be flexible in the types of information you share.** The union is entitled to a lot of information, and you are as well.
- **Try to understand what is really important to the other side.** Is it money, working conditions, something else? Of course, you need to develop your list of what is important to you as well.

- **Try to emphasize what you and the union can agree on.** There is plenty of time for discussing what you don't agree on that later.
- **Search for solutions.** Try to find strategies that meet yours and the union's needs.
- **Be flexible.** Sometimes the answer to the issue is not obvious and you may consider an approach that you have not used in the past.

I would always suggest you hire a professional to assist you in this process. The union will certainly be using one, and you should as well.

Contract Administration

Most of the attention thus far has been on the organization campaign and the collective bargaining process. This really only constitutes a small amount of the work that must be done. Administering the contract once it has been negotiated is by far the most time-consuming element of the union relationship.

Most of this effort will involve interpretation of the contract. While it may have seemed really clear at the time, unfortunately, history has shown that there will be disagreements after the fact with regard to language and interpretation. There will likely be issues that come up that were not anticipated at the time of the negotiation. When this occurs there is typically a grievance and arbitration procedure as shown below.

GRIEVANCE AND ARBITRATION PROCEDURE

Section 1: For the purpose of this Agreement, a grievance is defined as a written statement signed by an individual Employee, or by the Union, claiming a violation of the terms of this Agreement or a difference arising between the Company and an individual Employee or a number of Employees concerning the interpretation or application of any of the terms of this Agreement. A written warning or formal reprimand that could serve as a basis for discipline involving a loss of time or wages or termination, shall be removed from the Employee's file and cannot be used as a basis for discipline if the Employee has not received any other similar disciplinary action for a period of eighteen (18) months from the date of the warning or reprimand. Suspensions are not subject to removal.

Grievances shall be addressed promptly in the following manner, and if the time limits contained therein are not followed, the grievance shall be considered void and waived by the party seeking to bring such a grievance. No waiver of time limits shall be effective unless made in writing, nor shall such waiver be deemed precedent. The parties may mutually agree to expedite the procedures in the Steps below:

Step 1: Any Employee having a complaint or grievance under this Agreement shall first file a written grievance with his immediate supervisor. The aggrieved Employee or his Union Steward shall file the grievance with the aggrieved Employee's supervisor not later than ten (10) workdays after such occurrence is discovered by the Employee or the Union, or should have reasonably been discovered by the Employee or the Union. The immediate supervisor shall meet with the employee and/or his union steward within ten (10) workdays from the date the grievance was filed and respond to the employee or his union steward within ten (10) workdays after such meeting. If the immediate supervisor does not respond with such a written answer, the grievance shall be deemed denied by the Company.

Step 2: If the matter is not resolved with the aggrieved Employee's immediate supervisor, the grievance shall be submitted to the Department Head within five (5) workdays of the response to Step 1. Within ten (10) workdays from the receipt of such written grievance, the Department Head shall submit his answer in writing to the aggrieved Employee and the Union Steward. If the Department Head does not respond with such a written answer, the grievance shall be deemed denied by the Company.

Step 3: If the matter is not resolved with the Department Head, the grievance shall be submitted to the Human Resources Manager within five (5) workdays of the response to Step 2. Within ten (10) workdays from the receipt of such written grievance, the Human Resources Manager shall submit his answer in writing to the aggrieved Employee and the Union Steward. If the Human Resources Manager does not respond with such a written answer, the grievance shall be deemed denied by the Company.

Step 4: If the matter is not resolved in Step 3, the Union may request a meeting with the Site Director or his/her designee within ten (10) workdays after the rejection of the grievance by the Human Resources Manager or his designee. Such a meeting with the Site Director shall be conducted within ten (10) workdays after the request for the same. The Site Director shall submit her answer in writing to the Union within ten (10) workdays of the meeting with the Union. If the Site Director does not respond with such a written answer, the grievance shall be deemed denied by the Company.

Step 5: If the grievance is not resolved at Step 4, either party may move the grievance to arbitration by giving written notice of intent to arbitrate to the other party within twenty (20) workdays of the fourth-step response. The moving party shall notify the American Arbitration Association simultaneously with written notice to the other party of intent to arbitrate. The parties may jointly agree, but shall not be required to mediate any grievance prior to arbitration.

Section 2:   The arbitration hearing shall be conducted at a date, time, and place mutually convenient and agreed upon by all parties, including the Company and the Union.

Section 3:   The arbitrator shall have no power, right or authority to hear issues outside the scope of the issues by the parties, or to add to, delete, or modify in any manner the express terms of the Agreement or any supplementary Agreement.

Section 4:   Each party shall bear its own expense, including any witness expense, in presenting its case to the arbitrator. The losing party shall pay fees and expenses of the arbitrator. The minutes of any arbitration case may be recorded by a qualified reporter if either party so requests. The party requesting that the minutes be recorded shall pay the cost of the recording of said reporter, plus the cost of a copy of the minutes if requested. If the other party desires a copy of the minutes so recorded, he shall purchase such at his own expense and pay half of the reporter's cost.

Section 5:   For the purpose of this Article, Saturdays, Sundays and holidays shall be excluded in computing time periods, and shall not be considered as workdays.

Section 6:   It is a specific condition precedent to the processing of grievances that the time limits specified herein shall be strictly complied with and are jurisdictional unless waived mutually by the Union and the Company in writing. Therefore, any grievance not originated and processed within the time limits and in the manner provided herein shall be considered settled on the basis of the decision of the Company that was not appealed, the matter closed, and shall be final and binding on the parties and all affected Employees.

At the end of the day, the best policy is to pay attention to your employees' needs, provide a safe workplace for them, and pay them competitively. If you do all of this and follow some of my advice in this book, you should never have to refer to this chapter again.

Chapter 12
How to Manage Them Internationally

///

While I realize that many of you will not have international employees and this chapter may not apply to you, there may come a time when you decide to expand your operation. Whether this expansion comes in nearby Mexico or Canada or you move to Europe or Asia, managing international employees is somewhat different, and you need to be aware of the potential issues.

In this chapter, I will discuss two types of employees: locals you are relocating overseas and locals who are actually natives of the country you are operating in.

Relocating Expatriates

Locals who are relocated overseas are known as *expatriates* or *expats*. The selection of the expat is critically important, given that their annual costs can easily be two to three times their salary. While the proper selection criteria are beyond the scope of this book, here are a few things to consider:

Career Blockage
The assignment has to make sense from a career perspective. Often expats are sent overseas for two to three years and return to find a job that is not as "big" as they were used to. Repatriation is a

key to success. Upon their return, be sure their assignment allows them to take advantage of their new skills.

Culture Shock

Far and away, this is the largest problem expats face. While some destinations like Asia obviously are very different culturally, even Europe or Canada can offer challenges. It takes six to twelve months for most expats to adapt to their local setting. If you have long-term expats, the culture shock can also occur when they return to the US. Repatriation is important here as well.

Lack of Pre-Departure Cross-Cultural Training

You really cannot pick someone for an overseas assignment and just send them. Well, you can, but your chances of a successful outcome are very low. This is particularly true if the expat is bringing family along. You need to invest in pre-departure training. There are a number of excellent resources for you to use. Check out the following website: http://rw-3.com/?gclid=CKfnovTZzqYCFUpJ2g oddH8YIw.

Overemphasis on Technical Qualifications

While I understand that you may have picked this person because of technical skills that are critical to the assignment that may also be the reason he or she fails. We have all seen technical people promoted to leadership positions with less than stellar results. This is a problem that is more pronounced on overseas assignments.

Family Problems

The number-one reason for overseas-assignment failure is family-adjustment problems. While this cannot be totally eliminated, with some advance work in the selection process and proper orientation before leaving, your chances of a successful assignment increase dramatically.

Compensation

Be sure to explain the package thoroughly, because it will be complicated. Everything should be in writing and as clear and concise as possible. What will be covered? Housing? The kids' school? A car? Know the norms of where you are sending your employee and what is feasible and what is not. A pre-move trip is a must in my view. This should include the family as well.

Working with the Local Nationals

Over time, most organizations replace all or most of their expats with local nationals. Managing local employees is more complex than what you normally experience with expats. Again, the scope of this book prohibits a discussion of every region and country. Having said that, I would like to provide some general rules in dealing with your overseas employees.

Rule #1: Think Globally, Manage Locally

This is most important when we talk about compensation and benefits, but in general, while it is okay to bring your culture to other countries, you may have to make modifications in order to achieve success. For example, pay for performance, while standard in North America, is not accepted in many parts of Asia. I can remember discussing this concept with my leadership in Malaysia only to be told that they would prefer no increase at all than having to make these tough decisions.

Rule #2: Don't Believe Everything You Hear

Local nationals, while well meaning, will tend to tell you what you cannot do rather than what you can do. This is particularly true if they don't like your idea. For example, when closing my German sales office, I was told I couldn't layoff a twenty-year sales representative because of his tenure and age. When I started to drill down (after securing expert legal advice), it turned out I could — but was then told I would have to pay him until his normal retirement date, which was ten years away! The bottom line is that he was removed for eighteen months of severance, which may seem excessive in the US but is not uncommon in Europe. Things can be done, so don't accept a *no* at face value.

Rule #3: Don't Fall into the Religion Trap

Muslims are required to pray five times a day, but that doesn't mean they have to do all of them at work. When I first arrived in Malaysia, I was told that we were suffering severe productivity problems in a thousand-person facility because of the constant work and prayer breaks. It turns out that a little negotiation can go a long way. For the $50,000 cost of remodeling two prayer rooms, we were able to limit prayer breaks to the lunch and normal break times with the first and last ones at home. The investment in the prayer room was repaid in a couple of months. Do your own research, and you may be surprised what you find.

Rule #4: The Paradigm May Be Different There

Many of the most eye-opening experiences I have had have occurred in Malaysia. When I first arrived, we realized that we needed to do a reduction in force. At the time, the economy was very good, and the employees could get another job in a heartbeat. That, coupled with excellent government-mandated severance pay, meant the ones angry with us were the ones who had to stay! They actually wanted to get laid off. Go figure. Never assume that the US paradigm is the same everywhere.

Rule #5: You Really Can Hold Them Accountable

In developing countries, there is often the view that good enough is okay because they really can't do any better. This usually comes from your tired, burned-out expat who simply is tired of the fight. Working in Mexico for fifteen years convinced me that while it is indeed difficult, you can hold foreign workers to US standards. Accountability in much of the world is a difficult concept, but like any workforce, they can be trained. If the standards are set and training is provided, any workforce can be held to the required standard. If not, get out of that county and move someplace else.

Rule #6: People Are People

Over the fifteen years I worked overseas, this conclusion is the most obvious. Are they different? You bet. Are they from a foreign planet? Absolutely not. Getting to know them is the best way to understand their culture and way of thinking. I tried to visit their homes when possible, meet spouses and children and generally tried to understand why they think the way they do. Generally, if you are willing to share your life and show vulnerability, you will make great friends who will share their culture with you.

Interestingly enough there is not a lot of difference in hiring someone in the US vs. the rest of the world. Internet advertising is still used. Interviewing is the same. Background checks are subject to more privacy restrictions in some areas, but overall you will not find a lot of differences. There is also very little difference in making those new hires feel at home. Obviously, paperwork requirements are different, but sharing the overall culture and using a mentor is still a good idea.

Measuring job performance is an area where you will have to think globally but manage locally. While legally there is usually not much stopping you from using the same system and forms, you may find resistance and lack of understanding if you don't tailor your process to local norms. I go back to the idea of pay for performance in Malaysia as an example. Ultimately, after much discussion and training, the employees moved to the corporate system. I wonder, looking back, if there might not have been a better way to get to the same place. Overall, you will need to consider local culture and determine the appropriate style for managing performance.

Thinking locally is also the key in the area of compensation. One mistake many managers make is attempting to convert local salaries into dollars and pay according to a US standard. This is a mistake, because employees' pay in dollars bears no relationship to their local cost of living. People in other countries are paid in their local currency and live in their local currency, so the real question is whether they are paid a competitive local rate. The process of surveying is done exactly the same as in the US. Another area that can cause Americans confusion is the level of bonuses paid. By and large, US bonuses as the percentage of total compensation are higher than most countries. In many parts of the world, this percentage can be much less, making it difficult to compensate on the basis of performance. When this is true, it is best to respect the local custom.

When it comes to selecting a benefits program, I have good news: for the most part, you don't need to. Most of the world has health care provided or at least subsidized by the government, which takes this chore off your plate. You may want to look at a medical supplement plan that allows certain people to bypass the government system. This is very common for management-level employees. Life insurance is also a big deal in much of the world. Don't be surprised if you see five to eight times annual salary as a standard offering vs. the three to five times annual salary you would see in the US. Overall, though, this will be the least of your problems.

Oddly enough, dealing with employees' issues is also a bit easier in most of the world, but only because there are a series of very strict rules all employers need to abide by. Again, this will vary by region and country. In Europe, you have a virtual playbook of how to handle disciplinary problems. This is the good news. The bad news is that it is extraordinarily difficult to fire someone, and even a layoff is much more costly than in the US in terms of severance.

With all of the rules and regulations, you should be able to stay out of legal trouble. In many regions, though, there is a separate labor court that deals just with employee issues. For the most part, these courts are very employee-centric, which should not be a big surprise.

The training process abroad is virtually the same as in the US, although you need to be a bit sensitive to the culture. For example, when I train large groups, I like to encourage participation by tossing a piece of candy to the participants when they share or answer a question. While conducting a training program in Malaysia, at the first break of the day the manufacturing manager came up to inform me that throwing things at people was considered rude in their culture. Of course I was crushed, but then he said, "But understand, we still want the candy. Just hand it to us." You may also find these employees less willing to share individually than in the US. Overall, though, I have found most cultures to be very interested in Western training techniques.

Training and hiring the right person are particularly important abroad, because terminating employees can be painful and take a long time. The best way to describe this is to pretend the entire workforce is in a union, and in some countries that is true. Again, it is process, process, and more process. Follow the rules and you should be okay; deviate and the workday just gets longer.

Chapter 13
What the Future Holds

//

During my thirty-year career in human resources, I have watched the evolution of the workplace in awe and amazement. In 1980, the two-cocktail lunch was still common and technology was limited to the telephone and copy machine. In the area of technology alone, if you had told me then that I could work on a thing called a computer with 24/7 access to the world on a thing called the Internet anywhere in the world, I would have thought you had one too many of the cocktails I mentioned. I thought it would be fun to predict what will happen over the next thirty years based on what I have seen to date and the trends I have seen going forward. If I am still around then, I will be eighty-four and hopefully working on another book with similar predictions. For those of you who are still around, give me a call and let's see how I did. Specifically I will discuss these predictions:

- No one needs to work anymore.
- Everybody and everything is protected.
- Unions are back in style.
- Lawsuits continue with the government's help.
- No one is in the office — where are they?
- The younger generations have taken over, and are they different!
- Work life and the family are keys to talent acquisition.

- Regulation is the lifeblood of the profession.
- Technology will be even more interesting.
- What is an employee, anyway?

Finally, I'll offer some websites and resources to help you keep up with these changes as they come.

No One Needs to Work Anymore

In 1980, the only ways to get out of work were to go on vacation, get sick, get hurt on the job, or die. Of course, you could add getting fired or "made redundant" as well, but of course those weren't your idea. Nationally and locally, the trend in the past thirty years has brought us things like:

1. The Family Medical Leave Act
2. The Americans with Disabilities Act
3. Military Leave
4. Pregnancy Disabilities Leave
5. Crime Victims Leave
6. Domestic Violence and Sexual Assault Victim Leave
7. Election Leave
8. Literacy Leave
9. Parent's Leave (for school or day-care activities, or when children are suspended from school)
10. Organ and Bone-Marrow Donation Leave
11. Kin Care Leaves

The list goes on and on. While many of these are unique to California where I live, do not be surprised if these begin to make their way eastward as so many California ideas have in the past.

So what is the point? For the most part, these are unpaid leaves with reasonable notice requirements. I believe you will see this change in the next thirty years. There is a national movement to require paid sick leave on a federal level. California has had a paid disability leave policy for a number of years, and I see this trend continuing. All this really means is increased costs and more opportunity for plaintiff attorneys to claim you retaliated against someone for taking their entitled leave. What is next? I don't know, but if you think of a reason not to come to work, there could be a legal leave in it.

Everybody and Everything Is Protected

I grew up with Title VII of the Civil Rights Act. You know, the one where you can't discriminate because of race, color, national origin, and so on. Twenty years ago when I was teaching at the University of Redlands, I predicted that homosexual and transgendered people would become protected groups. Most of my students at the time didn't believe me, but here we are. We also have protections for whistleblowers, people with HIV, and most religions. Depending on your political point of view, these are either good or bad groups to include. I am not making a judgment other than to predict that this list will grow over the next thirty years, and with each addition to the list will arise a new opportunity for plaintiff attorneys.

The problem here is not that people are protected but rather the burden of proof in our administrative agencies, such as the EEOC and similar state agencies. To some extent, this is true of the court systems as well. The burden of proving that you didn't discriminate falls squarely on the shoulder of the employer, and the plaintiff's burden is minimal at best. Saying "I was discriminated against because I am a _____" should not be enough, but unfortunately it often is, to the detriment of the employer community.

Unions Are Back in Style

The current Obama administration is a big advocate of unions and the Employee Free Choice Act, which to date has not passed either houses of Congress. Given the current political climate, it may not pass soon, but trust me, someday it will. So what does this mean?

The Employee Free Choice Act (EFCA) is pending legislation that will fundamentally change how employers deal with unions. This proposed legislation will make it *much* easier for unions to organize your workforce and provide for severe penalties if you commit an unfair labor practice.

In today's labor environment, unions must secure signatures from 30 percent of the workforce on interest cards. Once this is completed, the union can petition the employer for recognition. The employer will usually want to hold a secret election and has several weeks to make its case for why the employees are better off without the union. The union wins if it secures 50 percent plus one of the vote at this secret election, and the employer is then required to bargain in good faith. EFCA changes this process in a couple of fundamental ways:

- If a majority of employees sign union authorization cards, the National Labor Relations Board (NLRB) can certify the bargaining unit *without* a chance for the employer to hold a secret election.

- There are also stricter penalties for employers who violate provisions of the National Labor Relations Act (NLRA). The bill would provide for civil fines of up to $20,000 per violation against employers found to have willfully or repeatedly violated employees' rights during an organizing campaign or first contract drive. Currently there are no civil fines for violations.

- There are new sets of mediation and arbitration procedures when a contract cannot be reached. The bill provides that if an employer and a union are engaged in bargaining for their first contract and are unable to reach agreement within ninety days, either party may refer the dispute to the Federal Mediation and Conciliation Service (FMCS) for mediation. If the FMCS is unable to bring the parties to agreement after thirty days of mediation, the dispute will be referred to arbitration and the results of the arbitration shall be binding on the parties for two years. The union and employer may extend any deadlines or time limits.

The bill was cosponsored by our current Secretary of Labor and is supported by President Obama, who said, "I support this bill because in order to restore a sense of shared prosperity and security, we need to help working Americans exercise their right to organize under a fair and free process and bargain for their fair share of the wealth our country creates."

Lawsuits Continue with the Government's Help

The Trial Lawyers Association is one of the most powerful interest groups in the country. It is said that in California, they and the public employees' unions really run the state. So what does that mean? Previously I discussed the various tools that plaintiff's attorneys use to stay in business. The most recent example is the issue of retaliation. If an employee complains about anything, there is a potential retaliation claim there for the filing. Another trend I believe you will see in the next few years is definition and regulation of bullies in the workplace. Currently this is not really a recognized cause of action, but in the next few years I predict it will become the next sexual harassment bonanza for plaintiff attorneys. So the real question is, will the government help? So far, the answer has been yes, with continued attacks on arbitration agreements as a prime example.

My only hope — and things would have to change a great deal to see this happen — would be the establishment of a separate court system for employment-related issues similar to what you see in Europe. I believe this would lead to faster resolution of employment-related cases, with fewer large awards because of the absence of juries. This system would function very much like a national arbitration system and resolve employee complaints quickly and in a far less expensive way than a court case.

No One Is In the Office — Where Are They?

I mentioned the tremendous growth of technology over the past thirty years. This has allowed many jobs to be done from home. I believe this will continue to be the wave of the future, due in part to the general green movement. I would also not be surprised to see legislation requiring an employer to allow an employee to telecommute unless it can be shown to be detrimental to the business. I know that sounds far-fetched, but let's chat again in thirty years.

What does this mean to your business? I believe it fundamentally alters the concept of management. No longer can we manage by observation. Now we will need to manage on the basis of productivity. Not a bad thing in my opinion, but many of our current leaders will find this approach far more challenging.

The Younger Generations Have Taken
Over, and Are They Different!

I remember fondly when I was the kid in the office. The difference between then and now was that I was the baby boomer and there was only one generation older than me that actually had a name or had been studied. Now we have Generation X, Generation Y, and the up-and-coming millennium generation. These along with the baby-boom generation have been widely studied, and their differences well documented. I believe their styles will clearly dictate what will occur over the next thirty years and fundamentally alter how work is done. This will be fun to watch, as I currently work with all four and the differences are profound.

Work Life and the Family Are Keys to Talent Acquisition

The old adage of all work and no play does not play with today's workforce. Work-life balance — a term I first heard in the 1990s — is real today. One of the ways that the Gen X, Gen Y, and Millennials will make their voices heard is in the area of work-life balance. They are not content to come into the office everyday from eight to five and work weekends as well. They are looking for more flexibility and ability to spend quality time with their families. What does this mean? Talent acquisition will change, and the winner will be those sensitive to these issues. Top talent will gravitate to those employers who understand and put practices into place that support the balance between work and home.

Regulation Is the Lifeblood of the Profession

Regulation will continue to be an issue in the human resources profession. Generally, the speed and depth of regulation depends on the political party in power at the time. The Obama administration has proposed or implemented more regulations in two-plus years than President Bush did in eight. This is the reality that human resources lives with, and the type and content of that regulation will continue to grow over the next few years.

Technology Will Be Even More Interesting

I am probably one of the least technical guys in the world and the last one to make any predictions about technology in the future. I can't even begin to imagine what we will see in the next thirty years, but I can predict the impact it will have on future generations. Baby boomers have been very impacted by technology, and in some cases have not made the transition smoothly. Will that happen in the future? I suspect so, although the current generations are more technology savvy. But at the end of the day, change is still change and difficult for many to accept.

What Is an Employee, Anyway?

This may seem like a strange question coming from a human resources professional. While we will always have employees, I believe we will also see many variations on that theme. The contingency workforce will expand dramatically, and more and more people will see themselves as free agents moving from one employer to another on a contractual basis. The days of working for a company for forty years and getting the gold watch are gone. For the new generation of human resource leaders, managing this type of workforce will definitely be a challenge. The emphasis will be on attracting the right talent rather than on keeping them forever.

Here are some useful websites to help you manage through this maze of human resources.

Organization	Website
Department of Labor	www.dol.gov
Equal Employment Opportunity Commission	www.eeoc.gov
Society for Human Resources Management	www.shrm.org
American Society for Training and Development	www.astd.org
World at Work	www.worldatwork.org

National Human Resources Association	www.humanresources.org
Economic Research Institute	www.eridlc.com
Employee Benefit Research Institute	www.ebri.org
HR Magazine	www.shrm.org
Workforce	www.workforce.com

Chapter 14
So You Thought It Was Okay to What?

//

I have been amazed at what some folks think passes for acceptable behavior in the workplace. With so many stories to tell and so little space, I thought I would group these stories into four categories:

1. Interpersonal issues among employees
2. Social media and technology
3. Ways to "beat the system"
4. Alcohol, drugs, and safety

Just for fun, I've also included some travel stories of passenger mistreatment that make you wonder what the airlines are thinking.

Interpersonal Issues

The workplace is made up of human beings, and as such, many unpredictable things can occur. These interpersonal issues can lead to some strange situations. In the early stages of my career, the concept of sexual harassment was just becoming accepted, and little case law existed. So what do you do when a very attractive woman who has a job that consists of installing computers, cables, printers, and the like chooses to wear microminis to work? In those days, the guys in the shop would whistle and hoot and holler. This is easy to deal with, and once the guys understood the rules and she understood the dress code, I thought there would be no problem. Unfortunately, a few weeks later she had enhancement surgery, and as a result, the minidresses became even more micro. When the general manager of the facility heard about her "new look," he raced upstairs to her work area and pronounced for all the world to hear, "Where is she? I want to see them." Fortunately, no lawsuit followed.

Over time, we also seem to have grown sensitive to smells. There are, of course, good and bad smells, but for some people perfume can be as offensive as body odor. On more than one occasion, I have had to address both issues, and many times I find the BO problem to be cultural. Simply telling an employee to bathe more frequently and use deodorant does not always solve the problem. Often you have to overcome decades of behavior and strong cultural ties.

Culture can also be exhibited in other ways. In the early 1980s when the refugees from Southeast Asia were still relocating in the United States, the relations between some groups were still very strained. Many times fights would break out between these groups who had been enemies at home. I remember one specific example of a Vietnamese employee chasing a Cambodian around the factory with a belt in his hand. Fortunately, he was subdued before he could do much damage.

Affairs in the workplace have been a problem for as long as men and women have worked together. For the most part, these come and go and run their course, but occasionally problems arise. I remember one female manager who was quite smitten with a security guard and began an affair worthy of the movie *Fatal Attraction*. When the relationship fizzled, she became quite angry and the stalking began. Finally, in fear of finding a bunny rabbit in a pot on his stove, he complained of the harassment and reported the problem to human resources. The investigation turned up over a thousand e-mails expressing her love and devotion, sent in sequences one or two minutes apart. The final straw was the naked pictures she sent on the company e-mail. Yuck!

As disturbing as that was, my favorite in this category was the enterprising young man who decided to run a brothel out of his RV in the company parking lot. His defense? Well, they were doing it on breaks and at lunch, not during working time.

Social Media and Technology

As time goes on, interpersonal issues in the workplace have been complicated by the use of social media and technology. While I think Facebook, texting, Twitter, and other such services are wonderful advancements in communication, in the workplace they can be problematic. When computers became prevalent in the 1990s, suddenly we had to deal with online pornography. Policies were developed, blocks put on, but nothing can really dampen the human spirit and the need to see dirty pictures. One of my customers runs education and training facilities for young people, and staff members are not allowed to date, flirt, or otherwise fraternize with the students. Imagine my surprise one day to open my cell phone and see a picture of male genitalia attached to a text message. Fortunately, there was an explanation, and this was part of an ongoing investigation. The text had evidently been circulated among many students and finally ended up in the HR manager's possession.

Facebook relationships can be difficult as well. On many occasions, we have had to remind employees that unless they take special precautions, Facebook postings are available for most anyone to see. Photos of our senior leaders plastered is not really the kind of image we would like to present on Facebook. Don't get me wrong — what you do on your own time for the most part is your business, but when the reputation of the company is damaged, this becomes a work-related issue.

Facebook communication can be a problem outside of the drinking and dating scene as well. This is also true of texting and Twitter. I think back on the employee who was playing with Facebook for hours at work, only to forget that her boss was one of her friends. Imagine her surprise when he realized what he was really paying her to do. Or consider the employee who texted her friends about how much she hated her boss, only to push the wrong button and send him the same text. Oops.

Ways to "Beat the System"

Employees can also be very entrepreneurial. Perhaps a better way to say this is that they feel a need to "beat the system." We once terminated an employee for running a catering business out of my customer's kitchen, which would have been okay if it had been the customer's catering business. This employee became indignant when terminated and felt she had the right to use these facilities any way she pleased. Go figure.

Don't have a car? No problem — borrow the company car and use it for personal business. This might not have been a problem had the employee not run it into a ditch on the way back to the office. Theft isn't limited to cars in many cases. I have had employees steal just about everything, but the best was the gentleman who tried to leave the property with a pickup truck full of copper wire that he had pulled from the buildings he was working on.

Perhaps my favorite story in this area is the employee who had stolen $6,000 worth of bottled water and coolers from a bottled-water company I worked for in the 1980s. When caught, he claimed to be "storing the material for us for free." What a guy!

Many employees don't realize that stealing time is the same as stealing money, and you can see this in the creative use of time cards and time clocks. I have had many employees clock in and out for other employees, but the most interesting was the employee who decided another employee had not worked as much as she claimed and helped her be honest by changing her time card to reflect this alternative view of time worked. This didn't end well for either one.

Falsifying documents is another big problem in many of the organizations I have worked with. Many of my clients are government contractors, and the penalties for incorrect documentation can be substantial. My favorite was the employee who didn't like the amount of tuition reimbursement offered, so she simply added to the amount she was supposed to get. As I write this, we are preparing for arbitration with her on this issue.

Alcohol, Drugs, and Safety

Perhaps the area where I have seen the most damage has been in the area of alcohol and drugs. Many careers have been severely damaged by drinking in the workplace, and more than once I have had to send someone home who either smelled of liquor or failed an alcohol test. A .05 at nine in the morning is a disturbing thing, and when the employee doesn't feel there is a problem I feel for him or her.

Drug use is similar but not always as blatant. I have one client who conducts post - accident drug testing, and one day I received a call that a cook had taken a nasty fall, hitting his head on the cement. He didn't want to go the health clinic for treatment because he felt sure he would fail the drug test. He finally did go, and surprise — he didn't fail the test. His admission, however, was trouble enough.

People's behaviors when it comes to safety are also interesting. You would think that your health and safety at work would be a top priority, but I have found this is not always the case. For example, does it seem like a good idea to go down a snow-covered hill in high heels? Or stand on a chair on one leg while hanging Christmas ornaments? Or mix two sets of chemicals together that cause you to pass out, and then do it again? The one that still has me shaking my head is the employee who was determined to use the restroom despite the tape blocking the door, the sign on the floor saying "just waxed, don't use," and the janitor telling her not to go in. Guess what? She did, she fell down, she broke her hip, and she caused a $50,000 workers' compensation claim. In my experience, 99 percent of accidents are preventable, but you have to pay attention to what you are doing and follow the rules.

What in the World Are They Thinking?

Finally, I want to share some travel stories with you. I have flown nearly three million miles over the years on various airlines, and I am constantly amazed at what this industry passes off as customer service. I was amused when I read about the Alec Baldwin incident on an American Airlines flight — he was thrown off the plane for refusing to stop playing Words With Friends on his iPad while waiting for takeoff — and I secretly had to admit I have been close to that behavior myself.

The first example involved a flight from Evansville, Indiana, to Chicago. This flight was on one of those mini-jets — you know, the ones with fifty seats or so. Well, the plane was leaving only half full, and there was a problem with one of the seats not reclining properly. Common sense would say, "Let's go, and we promise not to sit in the broken seat." After all, many of us had tight connections at O'Hare, so we were in a hurry. No such luck. The airline sent out a repairperson, and ninety minutes later, we were allowed to board. Was the seat fixed? Nope. Rather than fix the seat, the repairperson put yellow tape in the form of a perfect X on the seat. For this I missed my connection home.

Have you ever wondered about those little jets? I suppose the weight can be an issue, but once in Chicago I had a pilot announce that we would need to sit at the gate to burn some fuel since we were two pounds overweight. Yes, he really did say two pounds. Perhaps he meant two hundred, but that is not what he said. Are you serious? Take a six-pack of soda, throw it out the door, and let's go.

Pilots do say the darnedest things. On a flight from Miami to Los Angeles, we were delayed ninety minutes because the pilot said we were waiting for more cargo. Really? I am now flying on a cargo plane? I wrote a letter to the president of the airline requesting a cargo rate for 250 pounds (myself and my bag). After all, if I am now on a cargo flight, I shouldn't have to pay the passenger fare. Well, it turns out what he meant was that the cargo door needed repair. I guess I misunderstood.

Since I have discussed compensation in this book, I thought I would share a sad tale of customer service involving American Airlines. My wife and I were on a flight to London and the previous year had flown on United Airlines. Now on United, adult beverages were free even in coach class. On American, this was not the case. When I made this observation to my wife, the flight attendant overheard me and quite rudely declared that he had taken a 15 percent pay cut so I could fly American. Since this was a compensation teachable moment, I informed him that in reality, he had taken the pay reduction so *he* could continue to fly American. I had a lot of choices.

You really don't need to use the bathroom, do you? I was once on a flight from Chicago to Buffalo. We were delayed three hours while we waited for the crew to arrive. Once we had finally taken off, we were informed that the one and only bathroom was not working. Of course, nothing could have been done during the three-hour wait. What the heck, it is only a one-hour flight — just hold it.

Unions: love them or hate them? Having discussed unions in this book, I would like to share a not-so-proud union moment in Dallas. On my way home from a particularly grueling trip, I sat at the gate wondering why no one was loading our luggage. It turns out there was a shift change, and the employees actually stopped in mid-bag and left! Thirty minutes later, the next shift showed up and finished the job. Thank goodness for unions.

Perhaps the thing that really drives me crazy is the lack of honesty from airlines with respect to delays. I really can tell time. I don't know about you, but it drives me nuts when the airlines just can't tell the truth about when we are leaving. You have all been there. Sitting at the gate with the "on time" sign brightly lit, and yet no airplane is at the gate. Then all of a sudden, there is a fifteen-minute delay. Really? You can get the plane to the gate, unloaded, loaded, and taking off in fifteen minutes?

I think we are all relieved when we land after a long flight. We see the lights of the city when we arrive and start to think about the trip home, sleeping in our own bed, and so on. Have you ever landed but not landed? You know: get a few hundred feet off the runway only to have the pilot "punch it" and "take off." Fortunately, this has only happened to me twice. Once was in my home airport in Southern California, which was disconcerting enough. The really scary one, though, was in Bangalore, India, in the pitch-black middle of the night. Now, you would think some kind of explanation would be in order, right? Even an "oops, sorry" would do, but in India, apparently, silence is golden. No explanation, nothing. At least we got a sorry in Orange County.

They close the door, don't they? One time on a flight from Orange County to Chicago, we started down the runway, blasting away. Suddenly the pilot hit the brakes, and much like your car when you do the same, the effect is, let's say, mildly disconcerting. If you have never flown out of Orange County, the runway ends at the 73 Freeway. So my first thought as I watched my life flash before my eyes was, *Am I going to continue this commute on the freeway?* Oh, by the way, the problem was that the door wasn't fully closed.

And finally, do we have enough gas? Once on a flight from LAX to Hong Kong, I guess the 747 wasn't quite filled up. We left LAX the same way we always do, and I promptly fell asleep. I woke up with the plane landing and thought, *This is a bit strange*, since it didn't feel like we had gone far enough. Sure enough, we hadn't. The airline had miscalculated the wind speed, weight, fuel level, whatever, and we had to land in Beijing to fuel up. Imagine our surprise when, upon landing, we were surrounded by Chinese soldiers with their weapons held high. At least the flight attendants had a sense of humor about it and asked if anyone had a gas credit card they could use.

The Cycle Begins Again

//

Human resources management has been my life now for thirty years. When I say the cycle begins again, it is so true. People are hired, on-boarded, compensated, use their benefits, are trained, and yes, some get into trouble or simply cannot do the job and are terminated. In spite of this continuous cycle, we can all get better in selecting and leading people, and I hope in some small way this book will help you do just that. All of the things I talk about in the book are real and intended to illustrate (hopefully in some humorous way) the kinds of things you should expect when leading people.

I appreciate you taking the time to read this book and I always welcome feedback. You can reach me at jeffndi@aol.com.

About the Author

//

Jeff Stinson has been involved in the management and development of human capital for the past thirty years. Before founding GHRO Human Resources Outsourcing (GHRO), he ran a successful human resources consulting practice (JDS Consulting). Prior to JDS, Jeff functioned as a senior human resources executive for several companies, where he led human resource teams on three continents in the manufacturing, telecommunication, and software and entertainment industries. Jeff earned a Bachelor of Arts and Master of Arts degree in public administration from California State University, Fullerton. In addition to his university education, Jeff also holds designations as a senior professional in human resources (SPHR); Global professional in human resources (GPHR); certified compensation professional (CCP); Global remuneration professional (GRP); and certified benefits professional (CBP). He has also been an instructor at the Universities of Redlands, Chapman, and Phoenix since 1984, where he has taught a variety of courses in human resources management and leadership. Happily married for thirty-three years, Jeff and his spouse, Diane, reside in Irvine, California, where they enjoy travel, sports, and the theatre.

Global Human Resources Outsourcing

GHRO is a leader in providing outsourced HR services that help companies navigate risk, increase productivity and reduce the costs, complexities and administration burden related to employment. With nearly 100 years of HR experience, our dedicated staff has the expertise and flexibility to meet just about any HR challenge your company can encounter. Focus on what matters. Let GHRO take care of the rest.

GHRO – Global Human Resources Outsourcing
2465 Campus Drive
Irvine, CA 92612
888-308-0338
949-797-2001
949-797-2083
ghro@ghrogroup.com
www.ghrogroup.com

Global Human Resources Outsourcing (GHRO) is a division of Global, a 1st Flagship Company. Since 1964, Global has been achieving worldwide recognition for effective management and technical competency, and providing innovative solutions.